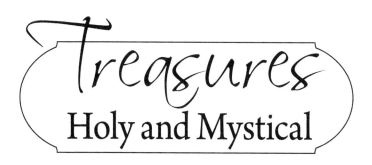

Treasures
Holy and Mystical

A Devotional Journey
for Today's Catholics

Philip Neri Powell, OP

Liguori
LIGUORI, MISSOURI

Imprimi Potest: Thomas D. Picton, C.Ss.R.
Provincial, Denver Province, The Redemptorists

Published by Liguori Publications, Liguori, Missouri
To order, call 800-325-9521 or visit www.liguori.org

Library of Congress Cataloging-in-Publication Data

Powell, Philip Neri.
  Treasures holy and mystical : a devotional journey for today's Catholics / Philip Neri
Powell. – 1st ed.
    p. cm.
  ISBN 978-0-7648-1913-1
  1. Catholic Church—Prayers and devotions. I. Title.

  BX2149.2.P688 2010
  242'.802—dc22

                                                                    2010009314

A list of additional sources and credits appears on pages 167 and 168.

Liguori Publications, a nonprofit corporation, is an apostolate of the Redemptorists.
To learn more about the Redemptorists, visit Redemptorists.com.

Printed in the United States of America
14 13 12 11 10   5 4 3 2 1
First Edition

Contents

Introduction

Anyone who prays will tell you that praying brings you closer to God. But what does it mean to be "closer to God"? If it's true that we "live and move and have our being" in God, how is it possible to get closer?

One answer: Prayer is the best way to clarify and improve awareness that we live and move and have our being in God. We don't actually move closer to God in prayer. God is always with us, but we are not always with God. Prayer sharpens *our sense* that God is always with us.

This excellent answer is one almost any good Catholic would give. But being proficient at prayer—being someone keenly aware of the presence of God—is only halfway to being what our tradition calls a *mystic.*

You may say you not only have no desire to be a mystic, but you have no vocation to living a mystic's life—an understandable response given what most people think it means to be a mystic, but it's also an unfortunate one. Being a mystic is what you've already agreed to become. By denying your call to the mystical life, you deny the very vocation you took at baptism.

What? You thought baptism was all about washing away original sin and becoming a member of the Church? Well, it is. And what do you think being a mystic is all about? Living in a cave, eating locusts and berries, and having visions of angels and such? Not so much.

However, that too could be the life of a mystic. It's just not the life most mystics live.

What we might want to call "ordinary mystics" live in the suburbs, have kids, go to work, pay bills, eat fast food, and occasionally have a vision of what the world would be like if we allowed God's love to prevail over the sin in our lives. Ordinary mystics pray on the run, ask God for help in desperation, cry out in grief and in joy, and even manage to share a moment or two of godly peace with fellow mystics at the office or at church. In other words, ordinary mystics lead extraordinary lives in the midst of the most mundane circumstances, for no other reason than practicing the good habit of trusting in God.

How radical is that! I mean, how like the call of Abraham or Moses or Samuel is it to go about the regular tasks of life trusting that everything you do and everything you say completes you as someone called to be Christ right where you are? It's radical. It goes to the root of your baptism, the very ground of who you were made to be.

When we pray, we place ourselves consciously, intentionally, purposefully in the subsisting presence of the divine so we might become more and more like the one we worship.

This is what it means to be a mystic. Or, at the very least, this is what it means to begin our adventure in becoming the best mystic we can be.

No one will doubt that prayer is the spiritual engine that moves us along the way toward God. Being fiercely aware of his presence in our lives is the jump-start we need to get us moving forward. But, as we have already noted, being aware of God isn't enough to fuel the sputtering engine of the reluctant mystic. Our prayer lives often flood out or stall from ill use or simply run out of gas.

How long can human flesh and blood stand in the awesome presence of God and fail to grow, fail to flourish, and still produce good fruit? Who among us hasn't stopped praying altogether because prayer became a mummer's play or vain repetition?

Of course, being with God is excellent beyond measure. But the purpose of prayer presupposes a willingness, an eagerness to improve, to develop, to be perfected in holiness. For this to happen, the ordinary mystic must be determined to become not only a presence with God but an actor for God, among others. In the same way that the mystic derives her spiritual progress from soaking in the Love that loves her, she must turn to her ordinary world and be the love that loves all creation.

Yes, exactly, the ordinary mystic is a sacrament of God's grace right where she is, wherever she is. Knowing this, our graceful prayer is the means we use to tune ourselves into becoming better instruments in the hands of the Divine Musician.

Traditionally, the Church has understood the mystic to be one who comes to mystery and lives there in enlightened ignorance; that is, once a person enters the mystery of God, takes up the work of prayer and ministry in his presence, and knows that complete knowledge of the divine is impossible, that person becomes a mystic.

As difficult as this path sounds, it is the path that all the baptized have committed themselves to. What else is the sacramental life of the Church but an immersion in the active presence of Divine Love for the sole purpose of preaching the Gospel to the world in word and deed?

I put together this book of mystical prayers in the hope that it will help you find the fuel you need to not only live and move in the presence of God, but also to begin an adventure toward finding perfection in Christ. When we move inward toward holiness, we simultaneously move outward toward a world starved for love and mercy.

The fist volume of this series, *Treasures Old and New,* was published last year. My purpose in composing the prayers in both books is to provide the earnest pray-er with the means of worshiping our Lord, learning more about our Catholic Tradition and, at the same time, pushing the adventurous soul toward the mystery of God, toward and beyond the limits of easy images and concepts.

Trusting fully that God's promises to us have already been fulfilled in Christ Jesus, our prayerful task is to live as if we were already in his presence, knowing him as we ourselves are known by him. And even though right now we cannot know him as he is, we can place our desire to know him in danger of fulfillment. Truly, this is what the ordinary mystic will risk: forgetting the idols of divinity to see him face-to-face.

Part One
The Novenas

Novena for Suffering
(Spe salvi)

In November 2007, Pope Benedict XVI published his encyclical letter *Spe salvi* (Saved in Hope), in which he teaches the Christian meaning of hope lived as a means of our salvation. In a section on suffering, our Holy Father challenges those who live by hope to suffer in such a way that their hope manifests itself as compassion for others, especially for those who suffer without hope. This novena draws you into a daily meditation on the meaning of suffering in light of Christian hope.

Opening Prayer

God of the Cross and Empty Tomb, you sent your only Son, Jesus Christ, to suffer for us and with us. He taught that we cannot follow him unless we follow him to the cross. Though we often fail to follow closely, we bear our crosses as we can. With the vigor you give us and by the example we have from your martyrs and saints, we lift our burdens and carry them, knowing we carry them always to you. Help us to not only suffer well but to suffer for others so our suffering will open the doors of hope. In Christ's name, we pray. Amen.

Scripture Reading

If I say, "Surely the darkness shall cover me,
*   and the light around me become night,"*
even the darkness is not dark to you; the night is as bright as
*   the day, for darkness is as light to you.*
For it was you who formed my inward parts;
*   you knit me together in my mother's womb.*
I praise you, for I am fearfully and wonderfully made.
*   Wonderful are your works; that I know very well.*
My frame was not hidden from you, when I was being made
*   in secret, intricately woven in the depths of the earth.*
Your eyes beheld my unformed substance.
*   In your book were written all the days that were formed*
*   for me, when none of them as yet existed.*
How weighty to me are your thoughts, O God!
*   How vast is the sum of them!*

PSALM 139:11–17

Reading

The true measure of humanity is essentially determined in relationship to suffering and to the sufferer. This holds true both for the individual and for society. A society unable to accept its suffering members and incapable of helping to share their suffering and to bear it inwardly through "com-passion" is a cruel and inhuman society (SS 38).

To suffer with the other and for others; to suffer for the sake of truth and justice; to suffer out of love and in order to become a person who truly loves—these are fundamental elements of humanity, and to abandon them would destroy man himself. Yet once again the question arises: are we capable of this? Is the other important enough to warrant my becoming, on his account, a person who suffers? Does truth matter to me enough to make suffering worthwhile? Is the promise of love so great that it justifies the gift of myself? In the history of humanity, it was the Christian faith that had the particular merit of bringing forth within man a new and deeper capacity for these kinds of suffering that are decisive for his humanity. The Christian faith has shown us that truth, justice and love are not simply ideals, but enormously weighty realities. It has shown us that God—Truth and Love in person—desired to suffer for us and with us. Bernard of Clairvaux coined the marvellous expression:...God cannot suffer, but he can suffer with. Man is worth so much to God that he himself became man in order to suffer with man in an utterly real way—in flesh and blood—as is revealed to us in the account of Jesus's Passion. Hence in all human suffering we are joined by one who experiences and carries that suffering with us; hence con-solatio is present in all suffering, the consolation of God's compassionate love—and so the star of hope rises (39).

Meditation

The most profound question for the Christian is this: do I care enough about my humanity—the divine gift of life as a person loved by God—to suffer for others?

Why should we define our humanity in terms of suffering for others? When we understand that suffering is not simply the experience of pain, but the gift of being able to give meaning to pain, we can see that we imitate the love of Christ on the cross when we lead others away from the mere feeling of hurt into a closer relationship with their created end.

How do we do this? Nothing is more despairing to someone in pain than to be abandoned, left to suffer alone. As our Holy Father makes clear, it is precisely because Christ suffered for us that we are able to suffer in kind for others.

Having been spared the final pain of endless death, we are freed by Christ to take on the work of loving those in pain so that they too might be able to find love and give their hurt meaning beyond crushing despair. Our Christian hope in the fulfillment of God's promises for eternal life is the engine that drives us to compassion. Looking faithfully at our end in Christ, we cannot be but moved to stand with those in pain to show them what we so clearly see.

Do I care enough about my humanity to suffer with others as Christ suffered for us?

Closing Prayer

God of Consolation, you are with us in our rejoicing and in our mourning. When we shout your praise, you hear us. When we cry for help, you hear us. In this time of great suffering among your people, hear us and help us. Give us the courage to look to the cross of your Christ, to learn to suffer well for the benefit of others. Our pain, our sorrow, our desolation will find their final meaning when we suffer as Christ suffered for us. And despite our sorrow, we live in your eternal hope, always breathing and speaking your Word. In Christ's name we pray. Amen.

Novena of the Word of God
(Dei verbum)

Our Holy Father, Pope Benedict XVI, has suggested that the wisdom of the Fathers of the Second Vatican Council is best understood when interpreted through the lens of that council's document *Dei verbum* (Dogmatic Constitution on Divine Revelation). This document defines and teaches how God has revealed himself to his creation and how that revelation is handed on through the Church that Christ founded on the faith of the apostles. The readings for each day of the novena are taken from *Dei verbum*. The biblical citations will lead you to a deeper understanding of God's Word.

Daily Opening Prayer

Lord God, in your goodness and wisdom you chose to reveal yourself and to make known to us the hidden purpose of your will, so that through your only Son, Christ Jesus—the Word made flesh—and in the Holy Spirit, the love you share, we may have access to you and come to share in your divine nature. Make us sharers in your Word; give us tongues of fire to preach your Good News; bring us to peace everlasting. Amen (adapted from *DV* 2).

Readings by Day

DAY ONE

Through this revelation, therefore, the invisible God (see Col. 1;15, 1 Tim. 1:17) out of the abundance of His love speaks to men as friends (see Ex. 33:11; John 15:14-15) and lives among them (see Bar. 3:38), so that He may invite and take them into fellowship with Himself. This plan of revelation is realized by deeds and words having in inner unity: the deeds wrought by God in the history of salvation manifest and confirm the teaching and realities signified by the words, while the words proclaim the deeds and clarify the mystery contained in them. By this revelation then, the deepest truth about God and the salvation of man shines out for our sake in Christ, who is both the mediator and the fullness of all revelation. (2)

DAY TWO

God, who through the Word creates all things (see John 1:3) and keeps them in existence, gives men an enduring witness to Himself in created realities (see Rom. 1:19-20). Planning to make known the way of heavenly salvation, He went further and from the start manifested Himself to our first parents. Then after their fall His promise of redemption aroused in them the hope of being saved (see Gen. 3:15) and from that time on He ceaselessly kept the human race in His care, to give eternal life to those who perseveringly do good in search of salvation (see Rom. 2:6-7). (3)

DAY THREE

Then, after speaking in many and varied ways through the prophets, "now at last in these days God has spoken to us in His Son" (Heb. 1:1-2). For He sent His Son, the eternal Word, who enlightens all men, so that He might dwell among men and tell them of the innermost being of God (see John 1:1-18). Jesus Christ, therefore, the Word made flesh, was sent as "a man to men." He "speaks the words of God" (John 3;34), and completes the work of salvation which His Father gave Him to do (see John 5:36; John 17:4). (4)

DAY FOUR

To see Jesus is to see His Father (John 14:9). For this reason Jesus perfected revelation by fulfilling it through his whole work of making Himself present and manifesting Himself: through His words and deeds, His signs and wonders, but especially through His death and glorious resurrection from the dead and final sending of the Spirit of truth. Moreover He confirmed with divine testimony what revelation proclaimed, that God is with us to free us from the darkness of sin and death, and to raise us up to life eternal. (4)

DAY FIVE

"The obedience of faith" (Rom. 13:26; see 1:5; 2 Cor 10:5-6) "is to be given to God who reveals, an obedience by which man commits his whole self freely to God, offering the full submission of intellect and will to God who reveals," and freely assenting to the truth revealed by Him. To make this act of faith, the grace of God and the interior help of the Holy Spirit must precede and assist, moving the heart and turning it to God, opening the eyes of the mind and giving "joy and ease to everyone in assenting to the truth and believing it." To bring about an ever deeper understanding of revelation the same Holy Spirit constantly brings faith to completion by His gifts. (5)

DAY SIX

Through divine revelation, God chose to show forth and communicate Himself and the eternal decisions of His will regarding the salvation of men. That is to say, He chose to share with them those divine treasures which totally transcend the understanding of the human mind. As a sacred synod has affirmed, God, the beginning and end of all things, can be known with certainty from created reality by the light of human reason (see Rom. 1:20); but teaches that it is through His revelation that those religious truths which are by their nature accessible to human reason can be known by all men with ease, with solid certitude and with no trace of error, even in this present state of the human race. (6)

DAY SEVEN

In His gracious goodness, God has seen to it that what He had revealed for the salvation of all nations would abide perpetually in its full integrity and be handed on to all generations. Therefore Christ the Lord in whom the full revelation of the supreme God is brought to completion (see Cor. 1:20; 3:13; 4:6), commissioned the Apostles to preach to all men that Gospel which is the source of all saving truth and moral teaching, and to impart to them heavenly gifts. This Gospel had been promised in former times through the prophets, and Christ Himself had fulfilled it and promulgated it with His lips. (7)

DAY EIGHT

[The commission to preach the Good News] was faithfully fulfilled by the Apostles who, by their oral preaching, by example, and by observances handed on what they had received from the lips of Christ, from living with Him, and from what He did, or what they had learned through the prompting of the Holy Spirit. The commission was fulfilled, too, by those Apostles and apostolic men who under the inspiration of the same Holy Spirit committed the message of salvation to writing. But in order to keep the Gospel forever whole and alive within the Church, the Apostles left bishops as their successors, "handing over" to them "the authority to teach in their own place." (7)

DAY NINE

And so the apostolic preaching, which is expressed in a special way in the inspired books, was to be preserved by an unending succession of preachers until the end of time. Therefore the Apostles, handing on what they themselves had received, warn the faithful to hold fast to the traditions which they have learned either by word of mouth or by letter (see 2 Thess. 2:15), and to fight in defense of the faith handed on once and for all (see Jude 1:3) Now what was handed on by the Apostles includes everything which contributes toward the holiness of life and increase in faith of the peoples of God; and so the Church, in her teaching, life and worship, perpetuates and hands on to all generations all that she herself is, all that she believes. (9)

Daily Scripture Reading

[Christ] was destined before the foundation of the world, but was revealed at the end of the ages for your sake. Through him you have come to trust in God, who raised him from the dead and gave him glory, so that your faith and hope are set on God. Now that you have purified your souls by your obedience to the truth so that you have genuine mutual love, love one another deeply from the heart. You have been born anew, not of perishable but of imperishable seed, through the living and enduring word of God. For "All flesh is like grass and all its glory like the flower of grass. The grass withers, and the flower falls, but the word of the Lord endures forever." That word is the good news that was announced to you.

1 PETER 1:20–25

Daily Meditation

God has revealed himself to us in three ways: through the Word of Scripture; through his Word spoken in creation; and through the Word made flesh, Jesus Christ. Christ himself gave his apostolic Body, the Church, the mission of preaching and teaching the truth of the Good News to the world. The Gospel is "handed on" (*tradere*) to each generation through the apostolic ministry of the bishops in communion with the pope, who is the successor of Peter. In his first letter, Peter tells us we've been born anew from "imperishable seed, through the living and abiding Word of God" (1 Peter 1:23).

How have I been "born anew" in the Church? How do I participate in handing on the Gospel? How am I a part of the Word of God that "remains forever"? If my hope is in God forever, how do I proclaim that hope in my daily life? How does my stewardship of his creation proclaim my reverence of and care for his word? How am I an apostle ("one sent out") in my daily life?

Daily Closing Prayer

Lord God—Father, Son, Holy Spirit—I offer these nine days of prayer to your glory so that you might work in me to bring about an ever-deeper understanding of your revelation in Scripture, creation, and Christ Jesus. You ceaselessly keep us in your care by bringing our faith to completion in the gifts you give us, especially the gift of your only begotten Son. Through his death, resurrection, and the sending of the Holy Spirit after his ascension, he brought to fruition what revelation has always proclaimed: that you are always with us to free us from the darkness of sin and death.

Open my heart, unstop my ears, free my tongue so I may know, hear, and speak your eternal Word to all the world. Amen.

Novena *Sacramentum Caritatis*

In October 2005 the bishops of the world gathered in Rome to reflect with one another and the Holy Father on the theme "The Eucharist: Source and Summit of the Church's Life and Mission." The presentations and discussions of this synod laid the groundwork for the Holy Father's postsynodal exhortation to the Church, *Sacramentum caritatis* (Sacrament of Charity).

About the purpose of this exhortation, Pope Benedict XVI writes, "Conscious of the immense patrimony of doctrine and discipline accumulated over the centuries with regard to this sacrament, I wish here to endorse the wishes expressed by the Synod Fathers by encouraging the Christian people to deepen their understanding of the relationship between the *eucharistic mystery,* the *liturgical action,* and the *new spiritual worship* which derives from the Eucharist as the *sacrament of charity*" (*SC* 5).

This novena includes short readings from the Holy Father's exhortation. The meditations and prayers will deepen your understanding of the eucharistic mystery and how this mystery leads you to charitable ministry. This novena is especially useful in a parish setting for adult lay formation.

Daily Opening Prayer

Through the intercession of the Blessed Virgin Mary, may the Holy Spirit kindle within me the same zeal experienced by the disciples on the road to Emmaus and renew in me a eucharistic wonder. Through the splendor of the Church's celebration of the Eucharist, may the sacramental signs of bread and wine, the Body and Blood of Christ—in all his infinite beauty—bring me and the Pilgrim Church closer to the mystery of God as we witness to the world in word and deed his unbounded love and mercy. Amen (adapted from *SC* 97).

DAY ONE

Christ makes a gift of himself

Opening Prayer

Reading

The sacrament of charity, the Holy Eucharist is the gift that Jesus Christ makes of himself, thus revealing to us God's infinite love for every man and woman. This wondrous sacrament makes manifest that "greater" love which led him to "lay down his life for his friends" (*Jn* 15:13). Jesus did indeed love them "to the end" (*Jn* 13:1). In those words the Evangelist introduces Christ's act of immense humility: before dying for us on the Cross, he tied a towel around himself and washed the feet of his disciples. In the same way, Jesus continues, in the sacrament of the Eucharist, to love us "to the end," even to offering us his body and his blood. What amazement must the Apostles have felt in witnessing what the Lord did and said during that Supper! What wonder must the eucharistic mystery also awaken in our own hearts! (*SC* 1)

Meditation

In the Eucharist, God's gift to us is the Body and Blood of his only Son, Jesus Christ. In an act of "immense humility," the Son took on human flesh and becomes man.

What do I find amazing in the Eucharist? What wonders do I experience? What does it mean for me to know Christ loves us "to the end"?

Closing Prayer

Lord Jesus, I give you thanks and praise for showing me the way to immense humility, the path to service in love and final sacrifice. Give me eyes to see and ears to hear the love you would show me and teach me in your Eucharist. Lead me to your table for the food of truth and out from your table to witness to the world in amazement and wonder. Amen.

DAY TWO

Christ is the food of truth

Opening Prayer

Reading

In the sacrament of the altar, the Lord meets us, men and women created in God's image and likeness (see *Gen* 1:27), and becomes our companion along the way. In this sacrament, the Lord truly becomes food for us, to satisfy our hunger for truth and freedom. Since only the truth can make us free (see *Jn* 8:32), Christ becomes for us the food of truth....Each of us has an innate and irrepressible desire for ultimate and definitive truth. The Lord Jesus, "the way, and the truth, and the life" (*Jn* 14:6), speaks to our thirsting, pilgrim hearts, our hearts yearning for the source of life, our hearts longing for truth. Jesus Christ is the Truth in person, drawing the world to himself....In the sacrament of the Eucharist, Jesus shows us in particular *the truth about the love* which is the very essence of God....Precisely because Christ has become for us the food of truth, the Church turns to every man and woman, inviting them freely to accept God's gift. (2)

Meditation

In the Eucharist, Christ is our "food of truth."

Do I hunger for the truth of the Gospel? Do I have an "irrepressible desire for truth"? How will I freely accept God's gift of truth in Christ Jesus?

Closing Prayer

Lord Jesus, in you I find the greatest truth of God's love for his creatures. Open my pilgrim heart to the Way you have shown us; help me search out and find the living waters for which I thirst. Draw me to you that I might become salt and light for the world. Amen.

DAY THREE

Christ's flesh is the bread of life

Opening Prayer

Reading

The first element of eucharistic faith is the mystery of God himself, trinitarian love....In the Eucharist Jesus does not give us a "thing," but himself; he offers his own body and pours out his own blood. He thus gives us the totality of his life and reveals the ultimate origin of this love. He is the eternal Son, given to us by the Father. In the Gospel we hear how Jesus, after feeding the crowds by multiplying the loaves and fishes, says to those who had followed him to the synagogue of Capernaum: "My Father gives you the true bread from heaven; for the bread of God is he who comes down from heaven, and gives life to the world" (*Jn* 6:32-33), and even identifies himself, his own flesh and blood, with that bread: "I am the living bread which came down from heaven; if anyone eats of this bread, he will live forever; and the bread which I shall give for the life of the world is my flesh" (*Jn* 6:51). (7)

Meditation

Jesus gives himself completely to us in the Eucharist. All we need for holiness is found in the celebration of his sacrifice for us.

Do I "take and eat" knowing that the Eucharist "reveals the ultimate origin of [Christ's] love"? How is Christ living bread for me? How will his Body and Blood feed me today?

Closing Prayer

Bread of Life, as I thirst for the living waters of your Gospel, I also hunger for the bread of heaven. Longing to be with you, I want nothing more than to be your faithful disciple, your servant and friend. In the Eucharist you show us God's trinitarian love, God himself, wholly present for our salvation. In my daily witness, help me feed the crowds longing for your Word. Amen.

DAY FOUR

Sharing in God's breath of life

Opening Prayer

Reading

The Eucharist reveals the loving plan that guides all of salvation history (see Eph 1:10; 3:8–11)....At creation itself, man was called to have some share in God's breath of life (see *Gen* 2:7). But it is in Christ, dead and risen, and in the outpouring of the Holy Spirit, given without measure (see *Jn* 3:34), that we have become sharers of God's inmost life. Jesus Christ, who "through the eternal Spirit offered himself without blemish to God" (Heb 9:14), makes us, in the gift of the Eucharist, sharers in God's own life. This is an absolutely free gift, the superabundant fulfilment of God's promises. The Church receives, celebrates and adores this gift in faithful obedience. The "mystery of faith" is thus a mystery of trinitarian love, a mystery in which we are called by grace to participate. We too should therefore exclaim with Saint Augustine: "If you see love, you see the Trinity." (8)

Meditation

As we breathe, we breathe with our Creator. In him we live and move and have our being. We have life without measure.

Do I live the mystery of faith, showing forth God's trinitarian love—the love of Father, Son, and Holy Spirit? How do I share with others the absolutely free gift of the Eucharist? How do I witness to the fact that I am a sharer of God's inmost life?

Closing Prayer

Blessed Trinity, when I see love, I see you. In Christ my deepest hope for life eternal is fulfilled. In faithful obedience, I receive, celebrate, and adore the gift of your Christ in the Eucharist. Give me the graces I need to live the mystery of faith, to participate lovingly, willingly in the superabundant life you have given me. Amen.

DAY FIVE

Radically renewed in Christ

Opening Prayer

Reading

In the Paschal Mystery, our deliverance from evil and death has taken place. In instituting the Eucharist, Jesus had spoken of the "new and eternal covenant" in the shedding of his blood (*Mt* 26:28; *Mk* 14:24; *Lk* 22:20). This, the ultimate purpose of his mission, was clear from the very beginning of his public life. Indeed, when, on the banks of the Jordan, John the Baptist saw Jesus coming towards him, he cried out: "Behold, the Lamb of God, who takes away the sin of the world" (*Jn* 1:29). It is significant that these same words are repeated at every celebration of Holy Mass, when the priest invites us to approach the altar: "This is *the Lamb of God* who takes away the sins of the world. Happy are those who are called to his supper." Jesus is the *true* paschal lamb who freely gave himself in sacrifice for us, and thus brought about the new and eternal covenant. The Eucharist contains this radical newness, which is offered to us again at every celebration. (9)

Meditation

Our renewal in holiness is the ultimate purpose of Christ's mission; therefore, at every celebration of the Eucharist we are offered the chance to be radically renewed, renewed at the root of our being.

How do I understand God's new and eternal covenant? What is my ultimate purpose in this covenant? Is it clear to those who live with me, work with me that my life proclaims, "Behold, the Lamb of God!"?

Closing Prayer

Lamb of God, you take away the sins of the world and renew us at the root of our being. I am indeed happy to be called to your supper. Drinking from the cup of your mercy and eating your bread of eternal life, I am made new. Help me live this covenant renewed as a prophet proclaiming your coming again. Amen.

DAY SIX

Our profound, radical, and universal salvation

Opening Prayer

Reading

[The Last Supper] took place within a ritual meal commemorating the foundational event of the people of Israel: their deliverance from slavery in Egypt. This ritual meal, which called for the sacrifice of lambs (see *Ex* 12:1–28, 43–51), was a remembrance of the past, but at the same time a prophetic remembrance, the proclamation of a deliverance yet to come. The people had come to realize that their earlier liberation was not definitive, for their history continued to be marked by slavery and sin. The remembrance of their ancient liberation thus expanded to the invocation and expectation of a yet more profound, radical, universal and definitive salvation. This is the context in which Jesus introduces the newness of his gift. In the prayer of praise, the *Berakah*, he does not simply thank the Father for the great events of past history, but also for his own "exaltation." In instituting the sacrament of the Eucharist, Jesus anticipates and makes present the sacrifice of the Cross and the victory of the resurrection. At the same time, he reveals that he himself is the *true* sacrificial lamb, destined in the Father's plan from the foundation of the world, as we read in *The First Letter of Peter* (see 1:18–20). By placing his gift in this context, Jesus shows the salvific meaning of his death and resurrection, a mystery which renews history and the whole cosmos. The institution of the Eucharist demonstrates how Jesus' death, for all its violence and absurdity, became in him a supreme act of love and mankind's definitive deliverance from evil. (10)

Meditation

Having been freed from slavery in Egypt, our ancestors in faith fled across the desert in search of their Promised Land. They marked their liberation with a feast. The Eucharist not only celebrates our liberation from slavery to sin, it is the means by which we are liberated.

How do I understand Christ as the paschal lamb of our feast, the victim of the sacrifice who saves me from sin? How does he turn his violent and absurd death into the greatest act of love for his friends, delivering us all from sin?

Closing Prayer

Lord, you freed your chosen people from the chains of slavery and set them in search of a promised land. In Christ, you renew human history and the whole cosmos. You show us the way to our freedom in this life and the eternal freedom of heaven. Untie the knots of sin that bind me; loose the chains of disobedience and oppression that burden me; lead me to the promised land of Christ's salvific love. Amen.

DAY SEVEN

The transfiguration of the entire world

Opening Prayer

Reading

Jesus thus brings his own radical *novum* to the ancient Hebrew sacrificial meal....The ancient rite has been brought to fulfilment and definitively surpassed by the loving gift of the incarnate Son of God. The food of truth, Christ sacrificed for our sake...By his command to "do this in remembrance of me" (*Lk* 22:19; *1 Cor* 11:25), he asks us to respond to his gift and to make it sacramentally present. In these words the Lord expresses, as it were, his expectation that the Church, born of his sacrifice, will receive this gift, developing under the guidance of the Holy Spirit the liturgical form of the sacrament. The remembrance of his perfect gift consists not in the mere repetition of the Last Supper, but in the Eucharist itself, that is, in the radical newness of Christian worship. In this way, Jesus left us the task of entering into his "hour."...The substantial conversion of bread and wine into his body and blood introduces within creation the principle of a radical change, a sort of "nuclear fission," to use an image familiar to us today, which penetrates to the heart of all being, a change meant to set off a process which transforms reality, a process leading ultimately to the transfiguration of the entire world, to the point where God will be all in all (see *1 Cor* 15:28). (11)

Meditation

The Body of Christ, the Church, is born and lives in the Eucharist. Having radically transformed the memorial Passover meal into a saving sacrifice, Christ commands us to remember and do likewise. With the Eucharist, the transfiguration of the whole of reality is accomplished.

How does the Eucharist transform my daily reality? How am I transfigured in the memorial sacrifice of the Mass? How am I a spark of the nuclear fission that penetrates to the heart of all being?

Closing Prayer

Christ Jesus, you are all in all. For me and the whole of creation, you are the transfiguring power of loving sacrifice. Liberated from the bonds of sin, I am freed to work with your gifts of compassion and care to serve those most in need. Help me be a spark that transforms the reality of this fallen world into a theater for the drama of salvation. Amen.

DAY EIGHT

Christ, who loves us first

Opening Prayer

Reading

Through the sacrament of the Eucharist Jesus draws the faithful into his "hour;" he shows us the bond that he willed to establish between himself and us, between his own person and the Church. Indeed, in the sacrifice of the Cross, Christ gave birth to the Church as his Bride and his body. The Fathers of the Church often meditated on the relationship between Eve's coming forth from the side of Adam as he slept (see *Gen* 2:21–23) and the coming forth of the new Eve, the Church, from the open side of Christ sleeping in death: from Christ's pierced side, John recounts, there came forth blood and water (see *Jn* 19:34), the symbol of the sacraments. A contemplative gaze "upon him whom they have pierced" (*Jn* 19:37) leads us to reflect on the causal connection between Christ's sacrifice, the Eucharist and the Church. The Church "draws her life from the Eucharist." Since the Eucharist makes present Christ's redeeming sacrifice, we must start by acknowledging that "there is a causal influence of the Eucharist at the Church's very origins." The Eucharist is Christ who gives himself to us and continually builds us up as his body. Hence, in the striking interplay between the Eucharist which builds up the Church, and the Church herself which "makes" the Eucharist, the primary causality is expressed in the first formula: the Church is able to celebrate and adore the mystery of Christ present in the Eucharist precisely because Christ first gave himself to her in the sacrifice of the Cross. The Church's ability to "make" the Eucharist is completely rooted in Christ's self-gift to her. Here we can see more clearly the meaning of Saint John's words: "he first loved us" (*1 Jn* 4:19). We too, at every celebration of the Eucharist, confess the primacy of Christ's gift. The causal influence of the Eucharist at the Church's origins definitively discloses both the chronological and ontological priority of the fact that it was Christ who loved us "first." For all eternity he remains the one who loves us first. (14)

Meditation

Christ is the Eucharist, and the Eucharist is the Church. Having loved us first by dying and rising, Christ gave us both the Church and Eucharist. Without Christ's self-gift on the cross and his resurrection, we would have neither the Church nor the Eucharist.

Do I love first? Do I draw my life from the celebration of the Eucharist? Am I a living Eucharist for others? How can I better submit myself to Christ to be drawn more closely to his hour?

Closing Prayer

Christ Jesus, you are the new Adam sent among us. From your pierced side on the cross flowed the blood and water that gave us your sacraments of grace. You are our cup of salvation, the food we need for our pilgrimage to heaven. You loved us first, giving us both the Church and the Eucharist. Stay with me, Lord, as I struggle to make my way, as I walk the dangerous road, carrying my cross behind you. Amen.

DAY NINE

Offer your body as witness

Opening Prayer

Reading

The first and fundamental mission that we receive from the [sacraments] we celebrate is that of bearing witness by our lives. The wonder we experience at the gift God has made to us in Christ gives new impulse to our lives and commits us to becoming witnesses of his love. We become witnesses when, through our actions, words and way of being, Another makes himself present. Witness could be described as the means by which the truth of God's love comes to men and women in history, inviting them to accept freely this radical newness. Through witness, God lays himself open to the risk of human freedom…Throughout the history of the Church, this has always been seen as the culmination of the new spiritual worship: "Offer your bodies" (Rom 12:1)….The Christian who offers his life in martyrdom enters into full communion with the Pasch of Jesus Christ and thus becomes Eucharist with him. Today too, the Church does not lack martyrs who offer the supreme witness to God's love. Even if the test of martyrdom is not asked of us, we know that worship pleasing to God demands that we should be inwardly prepared for it. (85)

Meditation

In the sacraments of the Church, God makes himself present to us, laying "himself open to the risk of human freedom" and empowering us to go out and make his presence known to the world. When we offer our bodies, our whole selves, as spiritual worship we commit ourselves to becoming witnesses of his love.

How do I make God's presence known in the world? What is my witness to the power of his love for me? Do I share the wonder of my salvation in word, thought, and deed?

Closing Prayer

Wondrous Lord, you gave us your only Son so we might not die but live. Wholly and truly yours, we work with your gifts to us to be faithful sons and daughters. To you I offer my body, my whole self, as spiritual worship. Help my every thought, word, and deed shine as a witness to the love you give me in Christ. Make me a witness to your wonder. Amen.

Novena of the Empty Tomb

The *Catechism of the Catholic Church* teaches us that the "discovery [of the empty tomb] by the disciples was the first step toward recognizing the very fact of the Resurrection" (640). We read in Luke 24:5-6 that the two figures in dazzling white ask those seeking after Jesus at his tomb, "Why do you look for the living among the dead? He is not here, but has risen." The emptied tomb was "an essential sign" to Christ's disciples and remains a sign to us that he is indeed risen from the dead.

Unlike Lazarus, who was restored to an "earthly life," Christ was claimed by the Father and brought to his right hand by the Holy Spirit. Along with the cross of the crucifixion, the empty tomb stands as one of the historical markers for the veracity of our faith and a sign of our eternal life to come. This novena will lead you to a better understanding of what the empty tomb means for us as followers of Christ—as those vowed by our baptism to follow him to death and back to our Father.

Daily Opening Prayer

Lord of Light and Giver of Peace, by raising Christ from his grave you brought to completion your plan for our redemption. I give you thanks and praise for the cross and for the empty tomb. May they stand in my heart and mind as signs of your marvelous love for creation. I do not seek the living among the dead, but rather eternal life in the death and resurrection of my Savior, Jesus Christ. Bring me and all your children—the whole of your creation—to your right hand in heaven that we may adore you face-to-face and live with you in perfect peace. In Christ's name I pray. Amen.

Readings by Day

DAY ONE

The cross and the empty tomb

The tomb is empty. It is a silent witness to the central event of human history: the Resurrection of our Lord Jesus Christ. For almost two thousand years the empty tomb has borne witness to the victory of Life over death. With the Apostles and Evangelists, with the Church of every time and place, we too bear witness and proclaim: "Christ is risen! Raised from the dead he will never die again; death no longer has power over him." (*Rom* 6:9)...The Resurrection of our Lord Jesus Christ is the sign that the Eternal Father is faithful to his promise and brings new life out of death: "the resurrection of the body and life everlasting". The mystery is clearly reflected in this ancient Church of the *Anástasis*, which contains both the empty tomb—the sign of the Resurrection, and Golgotha—the place of the Crucifixion. The good news of the Resurrection can never be separated from the mystery of the Cross.

POPE JOHN PAUL II

MASS IN THE CHURCH OF THE HOLY SEPULCHRE

JERUSALEM, 2000

DAY TWO

The empty tomb speaks

The lifeless body of Christ has been laid in the tomb. But the stone of the tomb is not the final seal on his work. The last word belongs not to falsehood, hatred and violence. The last word will be spoken by Love, which is stronger than death...The tomb is the last stage of Christ's dying through the whole course of his earthly life; *it is the sign of his supreme sacrifice* for us and for our salvation. Very soon this tomb will become *the first proclamation of praise and exaltation of the Son of God in the glory of the Father*...This vigil [in the Upper Room] will end with the meeting at the tomb, the empty tomb of the Saviour. Then the tomb, he silent witness of the Resurrection, will speak. The stone rolled back, the inner chamber empty, the cloths on the ground, this will be what John sees when he comes to the tomb with Peter: "he saw and he believed" (*Jn* 20:8). And with him *the Church believed*, and from that moment she never grows weary of communicating to the world this fundamental truth of her faith: "Christ has been raised from the dead, the first fruits of those who have fallen asleep" (*1 Cor* 15:20). The empty tomb is *the sign of the definitive victory* of truth over falsehood, of good over evil, of mercy over sin, of life over death. The empty tomb is *the sign of the hope* which "does not deceive" (*Rom* 5:5). "[Our] hope is full of immortality" (*Wis* 3:4).

POPE JOHN PAUL II

STATION 14, STATIONS OF THE CROSS 2000

DAY THREE

"He is not here" resounds!

At sunrise of the first day after the Sabbath, as recounted in the Gospel, some women go the sepulchre to honour the body of Jesus, who, having been crucified on Friday, was quickly wrapped in linen and placed in the tomb. They look for him, but they do not find him: *he is no longer in the place where he was laid. All that remains of him are the signs of the burial*: the empty tomb, the bindings, the linen shroud. The women, however, are disturbed by the sight of "a young man, dressed in a white robe", who proclaims to them: "he is risen, he is not here". This upsetting news, destined to change the course of history, from that moment on continues to resound from generation to generation: an ancient proclamation, yet always new. It resonates once again during this Easter Vigil, mother of all vigils, and it is spreading at this very moment throughout all the earth.

POPE JOHN PAUL II

EASTER VIGIL, 2003

DAY FOUR
The mystery of solitude

Jesus' solitude is not fruitless, quite the contrary: since it arises from an intimate union with the Father and the Spirit, it in turn creates communion in those who enter into a living relationship with it. Thus in his Passion Jesus encounters the fraternal support of the Cyrenean; he recognizes the consolation of the women disciples who have come up to Jerusalem with him; he opens the doors of his Kingdom to the centurion and to the good thief, who are able to look beyond appearances; he sees the beginnings of the community taking place at the foot of the cross, being formed by his mother and the beloved disciple. Finally, the precise moment of what seems to be his greatest solitude, when he is laid in the tomb, when his body is swallowed by the earth, becomes the passage towards a renewed cosmic community: having descended to the underworld, Jesus meets all of humanity in Adam and Eve, announces salvation to "the spirits in prison" (1 Pet 3:19) and re-establishes the community of paradise. For every disciple of Jesus Christ, participating in the Way of the Cross means entering into the mystery of solitude and communion experienced by our Master and Lord, accepting the will of the Father for us all, until we are able to see, beyond the suffering and death, the life without end that bursts forth from the pierced side and the empty tomb.

POPE JOHN PAUL II

INTRODUCTION, STATIONS OF THE CROSS 2004

ABBE ANDRE LOUF

DAY FIVE

The garden tomb

Jesus is dead. From his heart, pierced by the lance of the Roman soldier, flow blood and water: a mysterious image of the stream of the sacraments, Baptism and the Eucharist, by which the Church is constantly reborn from the opened heart of the Lord. Jesus' legs are not broken, like those of the two men crucified with him. He is thus revealed as the true Paschal lamb, not one of whose bones must be broken (*Es* 12:46). And now, at the end of his sufferings, it is clear that, for all the dismay which filled men's hearts, for all the power of hatred and cowardice, he was never alone. There are faithful ones who remain with him. Under the Cross stand Mary, his Mother, the sister of his Mother, Mary, Mary Magdalene and the disciple whom he loved... At Jesus's burial, the cemetery becomes a garden, the garden from which Adam was cast out when he abandoned the fullness of life, his Creator. The garden tomb symbolizes that the dominion of death is about to end... The hidden God continues to be the God of life, ever near. Even in the night of death, the Lord continues to be our Lord and Saviour. The Church of Jesus Christ, his new family, begins to take shape.

CARDINAL JOSEPH RATZINGER

STATION 13, STATIONS OF THE CROSS 2005

DAY SIX

It will happen again!

There are times when life seems like a long and dreary Holy Saturday. Everything seems over, the wicked seem to triumph, and evil appears more powerful than good. But faith enables us to see afar, it makes us glimpse the break of a new day on the other side of this day. Faith promises us that the final word belongs to God: to God alone! Faith is truly a little lamp, yet it is the only lamp that can light up the night of the world: and its lowly light blends with the light of a new day: the day of the Risen Christ. So the story does not end with the tomb, instead it bursts forth from the tomb: just as Jesus promised us, it happened, and it will happen again!

MEDITATION COMPOSED BY ARCHBISHOP ANGELO COMASTRI

STATION 14, STATIONS OF THE CROSS 2006

POPE BENEDICT XVI, PRESIDING

DAY SEVEN

What has happened?

The discussion, that began with the disciples, would therefore include the following questions: What happened there? What does it mean for us, for the whole world and for me personally? Above all: what happened? Jesus is no longer in the tomb. He is in a totally new life. But how could this happen? What forces were in operation? The crucial point is that this man Jesus was not alone, he was not an "I" closed in upon itself. He was one single reality with the living God, so closely united with him as to form one person with him. He found himself, so to speak, in an embrace with him who is life itself, an embrace not just on the emotional level, but one which included and permeated his being. his own life was not just his own, it was an existential communion with God, a "being taken up" into God, and hence it could not in reality be taken away from him. Out of love, he could allow himself to be killed, but precisely by doing so he broke the definitiveness of death, because in him the definitiveness of life was present. He was one single reality with indestructible life, in such a way that it burst forth anew through death.

POPE BENEDICT XVI

EASTER VIGIL, 2006

DAY EIGHT
We will find him

The Evangelist John recounts that when Peter and he heard Mary Magdalene's news, they ran to the sepulchre each trying as it were to outstrip the other (*Jn* 20:3 and following). The Fathers of the Church have seen in their haste to reach the empty tomb an exhortation to compete in the only legitimate race between believers: the competition in seeking Christ. And what can be said of Mary Magdalene? She stood weeping by the empty tomb with the sole desire to know where they had taken her Lord. She encounters him and only recognizes him when he calls her by name (*Jn* 20:11–18). If we seek the Lord with a simple and sincere mind, we too will find him; indeed, he himself will come to meet us; he will make us recognize him, he will call us by name, that is, he will admit us to the intimacy of his love.

POPE BENEDICT XVI

GENERAL AUDIENCE, OCTAVE OF EASTER, 2007

DAY NINE

We wait until the third day

Jesus chose not to come down alive from the Cross, but to rise from the tomb. True death, true silence, the Word of Life will be silent for three days. Let us imagine the shock experienced by our first parents upon seeing the lifeless body of Abel, the first victim of death. Let us think of Mary's sorrow as she embraces the body of Jesus, now reduced to a heap of wounds, more a worm than a man, no longer capable of returning his Mother's loving gaze. Now she must consign him to the cold stones of the tomb, after hastily washing him and laying him out. It only remains now to wait. How interminable that wait seems, until the third day.

MEDITATION COMPOSED BY CARDINAL JOSEPH ZEN ZE-KIUN

STATION 14, STATIONS OF THE CROSS 2008

POPE BENEDICT XVI, PRESIDING

Daily Meditation

Christ is with us always. The cross and the empty tomb stand as permanent signs of his death, resurrection, and his eternal presence among us. Ever-present, eternally accessible, he is not "there" but "here," here now, always. Those gathered at his feet under the cross formed the seed of his Church. They were among those who would find themselves set afire by the Holy Spirit at Pentecost. From the open mouth of the empty tomb, the Holy Spirit roared out and gave birth to the Church.

Does the empty tomb speak to me of his absence or his presence? his distance or his closeness? When I seek Christ and do not find him, where do I go? To whom or what do I go for consolation, wisdom, healing? How do I find my way back to Christ when I am lost? How can the empty tomb become my daily garden?

Daily Closing Prayer

God of Power and Might, you emptied Christ's tomb for the salvation of the world. From the barren rock of his grave, you gave us the fruitful gift of his Church. Help me to see that the tomb of my savior is the womb of my salvation, the ever-open doorway to eternal life with you. And as his emptied tomb speaks to the world of your love, make me a sign and a witness to your mercy in all I say and do. In holy name I pray. Amen.

Part Two

The Mystical Novenas

The word *mystical* is often used to describe spiritualities or religious practices that are simply enigmatic, unintelligible, or unnecessarily obscure and cryptic. Usually the more mystical a theory or practice, the less useful and connected to reality it is. No one would blame frustrated economists or physicists for describing their sometimes difficult-to-explain theories of money and black holes as mystical.

For Christians, the mystical is both a welcome reprieve from the mundane and a shock to our pride. In the face of the mystery we encounter in the divine, we stand in profound wonder—at the limits of our intellectual capacity. To remain too long at this edge can be dangerous. To refuse to even approach this mystery out of fear is foolish.

The three novenas that follow will draw you away from ordinary contemplation toward the liminal places between where you are and where you're capable of going. At the same time, they will challenge you to take this experience of mystery back to your ordinary life and contemplate ways of growing in holiness in the world you find yourself in.

The novena *via negativa* removes; the novena *via positiva* adds; and the novena *via Sophia* incorporates. To get the most from these devotions, use them in the order they appear in.

Novena *via Negativa*

What we know about God and can say about him is wholly imperfect. As imperfect creatures, our knowledge about the Perfect is necessarily incomplete, fragmented; for now, "we see in a mirror, dimly" (1 Corinthians 13:12). What we can claim to know has been revealed to us by Scripture, creation, and Christ Jesus. But even our understanding of this revelation is imperfect, and it will not be perfect until we see God "face to face."

The early Church Fathers developed a way of talking about God called *apophatic* theology, or the *via negativa*, "the way of negation." Rather than trying to talk about who and what God is (the *via positiva*), they talked about who and what God is *not*. Rightly concerned about the possibility of idolatry—making words, images, or things into God—the Fathers taught Christians to understand that language, images, and concepts describing or depicting God are wholly inadequate to the task of fully expressing the divine nature.

This novena challenges you to walk a bit with the *via negativa*, to travel a short while along the apophatic path to submit your potentially idolatrous language and images to a test against the ineffable glory of God.

Daily Opening Prayer

Ineffable God, your apostle and prophet the evangelist John teaches that no creature has seen you. Only your Son, who sits at your right side, has seen you, and he reveals you to all the world. Through his unique and final revelation we have a glimpse of all you are. Seen imperfectly and understood nearly not at all, we struggle to see and hear the fullness of your majesty with our words and images, our concepts and symbols. Though we cannot give words to all that is true in you, we want nothing more than to speak only truth about you. Move us beyond words, beyond images, beyond concepts. Fill us to our full capacity and show us all we lack. In Christ's name we pray. Amen.

Daily Closing Prayer

Lord God, defy our expectations and speak to us softly; show us all you are not. Reveal the unworthiness of what we know about you and hold us against your ineffable majesty. Deepen our ignorance that we might know the depths of your mystery. In Christ's name we pray. Amen.

Hymn to the Transcendence of God

How can I sing your Name, O Lord?
You are beyond all things of creation!
How can my words praise you, O Lord?
You are praised by no word of mine.
You alone are unsayable, O Lord!
though all that I say is from you.

How can my mind grasp you, O Lord?
You are grasped by no creature's mind.
You alone are unknowable, O Lord!
since all that is known is from you.
All those who preach and do not preach announce you.
All those who reason and do not reason abide by you.
All desires and all sufferings are given to you.
All things pray to you, and sing a silent hymn.
In you alone all things abide, to you all things together hurry.
For you are the end, the one, the all, the nothing, not one, not all.
Be gracious, O Lord, beyond all things!
For how else is it fitting to sing you?

DAY ONE

What are you doing here?

Daily Opening Prayer

Reading

[Threatened by Jezebel, Elijah was afraid] and fled for his life, and came to Beer-sheba, which belongs to Judah; he left his servant there. But he himself went a day's journey into the wilderness, and came and sat down under a solitary broom tree. He asked that he might die: "It is enough; now, O Lord, take away my life, for I am no better than my ancestors." Then he lay down under the broom tree and fell asleep. Suddenly an angel touched him and said to him, "Get up and eat"…. He ate and drank, and lay down again. The angel of the Lord came a second time, touched him, and said, "Get up and eat, otherwise the

journey will be too much for you." He got up, and ate and drank; then he went in the strength of that food forty days and forty nights to Horeb the mount of God.

At that place he came to a cave, and spent the night there. Then the word of the Lord came to him, saying, "What are you doing here, Elijah?" He answered, "I have been very zealous for the Lord, the God of hosts; for the Israelites have forsaken your covenant, thrown down your altars, and killed your prophets with the sword. I alone am left, and they are seeking my life, to take it away." He said, "Go out and stand on the mountain before the Lord, for the Lord is about to pass by." Now there was a great wind, so strong that it was splitting mountains and breaking rocks in pieces before the Lord, but the Lord was not in the wind; and after the wind an earthquake, but the Lord was not in the earthquake; and after the earthquake a fire, but the Lord was not in the fire; and after the fire a sound of sheer silence. When Elijah heard it, he wrapped his face in his mantle and went out and stood at the entrance of the cave. Then there came a voice to him that said, "What are you doing here, Elijah?"

1 KINGS 19:3–13

Meditation

Elijah hears a small, quiet voice asking, "What are you doing here, Elijah?" Expecting his Lord to speak in the lashing wind or the thundering earthquake or the blazing fire, Elijah is called by a tiny whisper. In the scarcity of the desert, afraid for his life and completely dependent on the generosity of the Lord, Elijah is challenged to answer a question none of us wants to hear.

What is my purpose? Defying expectation, this test doesn't come in a dramatic event nor is it delivered in a booming voice, but rather in a soft murmur, nearly a breeze. Why does God use a whisper to test Elijah and send him on his prophetic way?

Hymn to the Transcendent God

Closing Prayer

DAY TWO
Dwelling in unapproachable light

Opening Prayer

Reading

Pursue righteousness, godliness, faith, love, endurance, gentleness. Fight the good fight of the faith; take hold of the eternal life, to which you were called and for which you made the good confession in the presence of many witnesses.

In the presence of God, who gives life to all things, and of Christ Jesus, who in his testimony before Pontius Pilate made the good confession, I charge you to keep the commandment without spot or blame until the manifestation of our Lord Jesus Christ, which he will bring about at the right time—he who is the blessed and only Sovereign, the King of kings and Lord of lords. It is he alone who has immortality and dwells in unapproachable light, whom no one has ever seen or can see; to him be honor and eternal dominion. Amen.

1 TIMOTHY 6:11–16

Meditation

Does it strike you as odd that Timothy would exhort us to pursue righteousness by unflinchingly obeying the commandments of a king we've never seen nor will ever see? Is this what critics of the Christian faith call "blind obedience"? What difference is there between being blinded by the fathomless dark and blinded by an unapproachable light? If you've been baptized, you've "made the good confession in the presence of many witnesses," and this confession places you squarely in the light. Blinded or not, you're committed to the pursuit of righteousness.

Will I become the darkness? Or will I approach the unapproachable light and get as close as I can? How do I approach that which cannot be approached? How does the daily imitation of Christ equip me for the hike to light, the light I can never reach this side of heaven?

Hymn to the Transcendent God

Closing Prayer

DAY THREE

If the very soul grew silent

Opening Prayer

Reading

If the tumult of the flesh were silenced; and the phantoms of earth and waters and air were silenced; and the poles were silent as well; indeed, if the very soul grew silent to herself, and went beyond herself by not thinking of herself; if fancies and imaginary revelations were silenced; if every tongue and every sign and every transient thing…and if, having uttered this, they too should be silent, having stirred our ears to hear him who created them; and if then he alone spoke, not through them but by himself, that we might hear his word, not in fleshly tongue or angelic voice, nor sound of thunder, nor the obscurity of a parable, but might hear him…if we could hear him without these…we then with rapid thought might touch on that Eternal Wisdom which abides over all. And if this could be sustained, and other visions of a far different kind be taken away, and this one should so ravish and absorb and envelop its beholder in these inward joys that his life might be eternally like that one moment of knowledge which we now sighed after—would not *this* be the reality of the saying, "Enter into the joy of your Lord"?

SAINT AUGUSTINE

ADAPTED FROM *CONFESSIONS*, IX.10.25, TRANS. OUTLER

Meditation

Strip away the spoken word, the noise of music, the puzzles of the parable; silence the thunder, the roar of traffic, the rhythm of work; take away the picture, the statue, the prayer; remove it all, and hear God as if "he alone spoke" and then "enter into the joy of your Lord." Because we love God and want to grow closer to him, we sometimes allow "fancies and imaginary revelations" to accumulate, to spring up and thrive among the beauties of his revelation.

Perhaps out of devotional exuberance or a rush to claim an extraordinary experience of the divine, we create spiritual dramas, angelic conspiracies, and sometimes "other visions of a far different kind."

Insofar as these color our faith, they are welcome adornment. But when they become the object of our veneration, we fall into idolatry. Thus, Augustine firmly grounds our joy in hearing the Eternal Wisdom of God without distraction, decoration, or mediation so that our lives "might be eternally like that one moment of knowledge" breathed by Wisdom himself.

Is this possible for us while we live? Can we hear God's wisdom so pristinely, so clearly? Can I identify the layers of distraction—antique and novel—that I have placed between myself and God's Word?

Hymn to the Transcendent God

Closing Prayer

DAY FOUR

The soul's naked being

Opening Prayer

Reading

We read of one good man who was entreating God in his prayer and wanted to give him names. Then a brother said: "Be quiet—you are dishonoring God." We cannot find a single name we might give to God. Yet those names are permitted to us by which the saints have called him and which God consecrated with divine light and poured into all their hearts. And through these we should first learn how we ought to pray…Even if the soul contemplates God, either as God or an image or as a three, the soul lacks something. But if all images are detached from the soul, and it contemplates only the Simple One, then the soul's naked being finds the naked, formless being of the divine unity, which is there a being above being, accepting and reposing in itself…If I say: "God is a being," it is not true; he is a being transcending being and transcending nothingness…So be silent, and do not chatter about God; for when you do chatter about him, you are telling lies and sinning…If you can understand anything about him, it in no way belongs to him, and insofar as you understand anything about him, that brings you into incomprehension, and from incomprehension you arrive at brute stupidity…So if you do not wish to be brutish, do not understand the God who is beyond words.

MEISTER ECKHART IN *MEISTER ECKHART*, NN. 53 AND 83;

TRANS. COLLEDGE & MCGINN

Meditation

So, be silent. Do not chatter about God because anything we say will be a lie. Unless we come to the "soul's naked being" and meet "the naked, formless being of the divine unity," we will always speak—when we speak about God—in riddles and paradox, swerving inevitably around and away from the Simple One. And yet, we must pray; we must worship; we must talk to and about God so that our joy may be complete in a faithful witness to his boundless mercy.

God is certainly beyond our words. Can we speak about God *and* to God knowing full well that our speech is wholly deficient, entirely inadequate? What other choice do we have? We can sit in silence and witness with hushed awe. We can strip clean the altars of our mind and worship at bare stone. But even then we are seduced by an inextricable desire to shout or cry or laugh.

Can we—in the full bloom of our stupidity—both speak about God and to him and confess the stupidity of our speech, knowing and acknowledging the invincible limits of our creatureness? Isn't this what we call humility? What must I do to find my soul's naked being? What must I strip away, detach from, surrender, to find myself naked before the naked being of divine unity?

Hymn to the Transcendent God

Closing Prayer

DAY FIVE

The seeing that consists of not seeing

Opening Prayer

Reading

Scripture teaches…that religious knowledge comes at first to those who receive it as light. Therefore what is perceived to be contrary to religion is darkness, and the escape from darkness comes about when one participates in the light. But as the mind progresses and, through an ever greater and more perfect diligence, comes to apprehend reality, as it approaches more nearly to contemplation, it sees more clearly what of the divine nature is uncontemplated. For leaving behind everything that is observed, not only what sense comprehends but also what the intelligence thinks it sees, it keeps on penetrating deeper until by the intelligence's yearning for understanding it gains access to the invisible and the incomprehensible, and there it sees God. This is the true knowledge of what is sought; this is the seeing that consists in not seeing, because that which is sought transcends all knowledge, being separated on all sides by incomprehensibility as by a kind of darkness.

GREGORY OF NYSSA
LIFE OF MOSES, PAULIST PRESS, 1978

Meditation

We know that two apples added to two apples equals four apples. But what does it mean "to add"? What does it mean "to equal to"? Sense comprehends what is sensible and makes sense of what we see and hear and smell. Our words denote things and the relationships between and among these things. We count. We categorize. We organize and label. But do these ways of fitting things together, these ways of naming bring understanding? Can we "stand under" four apples and comprehend addition? Can we understand "God," "divinity," "transcendence," and see God? What is the light we receive when we receive religious knowledge?

In the darkness, we need light to see. Light generated by our own power will penetrate only so far (counting, naming, organizing). Standing in the light provided by our graced relationship to God, we see otherwise by not seeing at all.

In what ways do I trap my understanding of God and my relationship to him in my "seeing," my need to comprehend? What do I think my intelligence tells me about God? Do I follow this formula: Senses + Intelligence = Knowledge? Where is God in this formula?

Hymn to the Transcendent God

Closing Prayer

DAY SIX

No knowledge beyond our capacity

Opening Prayer

Reading

The uncreated Nature alone, which we acknowledge in [the Trinity] surpasses all significance of names. For this cause the Word, when he spoke of "the name" in giving us the Faith, did not add what this name is—for how could a name be found for that which is above every name? [Rather], to indicate the transcendent Nature, he gave authority to [a name that] our intelligence [could by our pious efforts discover] that name should be applied alike to Father, Son, and Holy Spirit, whether it be "the Good" or "the Incorruptible," whatever name each may think properly employed to indicate the undefiled Nature of Godhead. And by this [gift] the Word seems to me to lay down for us this law, that we are to be persuaded that the Divine Essence is ineffable and incomprehensible: for it is plain that the title of Father does not present to us the Essence, but only indicates the relation to the Son. It follows, then, that if it were possible for human nature to be taught the essence of God, he would not have suppressed the knowledge upon this matter. But as it is, by saying nothing concerning the Divine Essence, he showed that this knowledge is beyond our power, [because when we have learned all we are capable of learning], we stand in no need of the knowledge beyond our capacity. We have in the profession of faith delivered to us all that we need for our salvation. For to learn that he is the absolutely existent, together with Whom is declared the majesty of the Son [and the Spirit], is the fullest teaching of godliness.

GREGORY OF NYSSA

ADAPTED FROM *AGAINST EUNOMIUS*, II.3

Meditation

When do we know enough to be saved? How much learning must we do to find ourselves finally living in right relationship to God? We can learn facts, gather information, and disseminate knowledge. We can argue that this or that piece of information is true or false. We need solid data to make decisions about the economy, politics, nutrition—every decision we make, small and great—requires some sort of factual information.

What must we know to be saved? How much information we do need to know God? Gregory argues that we need nothing more than to know God exists. Everything a Christian requires to grow in holiness is contained in the Creed. But is the profession of faith properly informational, factual? A profession of faith is a confession of trust, an expression of fidelity and love.

No one can doubt that the Creeds of the Church show us the limits of the faith, but do they give us knowledge of God to our full capacity to know him? Do I have the capacity to learn and live a godly wisdom beyond the facts of the historical faith? At what point do facts, information, and knowledge become irrelevant to my relationship with God?

Hymn to the Transcendent God

Closing Prayer

DAY SEVEN

One thing to speak and another to know

Opening Prayer

Reading

No one has seen God at any time. The Only-begotten Son, who is in the bosom of the Father, he has declared him to us. God, therefore, is ineffable and incomprehensible. For no one knows the Father, save the Son, nor the Son, save the Father. And the Holy Spirit, too, so knows the things of God as the spirit of the man knows the things that are in him…God, however, did not leave us in absolute ignorance. God has implanted knowledge of his existence in all by nature. This creation, its maintenance and its government, proclaim the majesty of the Divine nature. Moreover, through the Law and the Prophets in former times, and afterwards through his Only-begotten Son, our Lord and God and Saviour Jesus Christ, he disclosed to us the knowledge of himself that was possible for us to know…It is necessary, therefore, that one who wishes to speak or to hear of God should understand clearly that in the doctrine of God and in the Incarnation, all things are neither unutterable nor utterable; neither all unknowable nor all knowable. Just as it is one thing to speak and another thing to know, the knowable belongs to one order, and the utterable to another. Many of the things relating to God, therefore, that are dimly understood cannot be put into fitting terms, but on things above us we cannot do otherwise than to express ourselves according to our limited capacity.

JOHN OF DAMASCUS

ADAPTED FROM *EXPOSITION OF THE ORTHODOX FAITH*, I.1, 2

Meditation

Physicists sometimes sound like mystics. When asked to explain black holes, quantum phenomena, or the possibility of time travel, these cutting-edge philosophers of the material world lapse into language and images reminiscent of the most esoteric gurus of transcendental experience.

They can be forgiven this unscientific lapse precisely because what they are trying to explain often involves concepts worked out in higher mathematics—systems of multidimensional geometries and calculus not easily translated into ordinary language. They can express what they believe to be true. According to their limited capacities, they can explain what they have discovered and what it means for how we see the universe.

Similarly, humble Christians will stand on truth and explain it within the constraints of human language and image, keeping a trusting eye focused on the horizon of revelation and understanding. This doesn't mean that what we believe to be true is rooted in sand. It means we're challenged to admit that "all things are neither unutterable nor utterable; neither all unknowable nor all knowable." Here is our chance to practice humility.

To what extent, if at all, have I made my words and concepts of the divine into idols, lifting my necessarily limited understanding to the level of absolute knowledge? Do I believe I say everything there is to say about God when I say everything I know about God?

Hymn to the Transcendent God

Closing Prayer

DAY EIGHT

Neither without being nor without life

Opening Prayer

Reading

Is it not more true to affirm that God is Life and Goodness than that God is air or stone; and must we not deny to God more emphatically the attributes of inebriation and wrath than the applications of human speech and thought? We therefore maintain that the universal and transcendent Cause of all things is neither without being nor without life, nor without reason or intelligence; nor is it a body, nor has it form or shape, quality, quantity or weight;... it needs no light; it suffers no change, corruption, division, privation or flux; none of these things can either be identified with or attributed to it.... Again, ascending yet higher, we maintain that it is neither soul nor intellect; nor has it imagination, opinion, reason or understanding; nor can it be expressed or conceived;... neither is it standing, nor moving, nor at rest; neither has it power nor is power, nor is light; neither does it live nor is it life; neither is it essence, nor eternity nor time; nor is it subject to intelligible contact; nor is it science nor truth, nor kingship nor wisdom; neither one nor oneness, nor godhead nor goodness;... nor can any affirmation or negation be applied to it, for although we may affirm or deny the things below it, we can neither affirm nor deny it, inasmuch as the all-perfect and unique Cause of all things transcends all affirmation, and the simple pre-eminence of Its absolute nature is outside of every negation, free from every limitation and beyond them all.

DIONYSIUS THE AEROPAGITE

MYSTICAL THEOLOGY, KESSLINGER PUBLISHING, 2005, 17–19

Meditation

What if our faith is more akin to poetry than math? For example, reflect on a world in which we communicate by negating qualities rather than positively asserting them. Rather than saying "my boss is tall," you say, "my boss is not short." Or go even further into negation: Rather than saying, "I have three children," you say, "I don't have four children." It's fairly easy to see here that simply negating a positive with its opposite doesn't render identical meaning.

Nor do we arrive at precision by excluding only one possibility while remaining open to all others. How long would it take you to buy a shirt if you told the salesperson, "I'm not looking for shoes"? Though terribly inconvenient for daily living, the *via negativa* is a solemn poetic path to God through practiced ignorance. Negation gives us a means of admitting in all humility our inability to capture and hold the divine in a prison of language.

Even as we praise God and give him thanks as our Father, we must know as well that he is not our Father. This is not a denial of truth, but rather a confession that our concept "father" cannot empty all God truly is. Surely this can cause us some anxiety. There is comfort in clearly stated, precisely formulated language.

As a Christian, am I supposed to be comforted by words?

Hymn to the Transcendent God

Closing Prayer

DAY NINE

Therefore, magnify the Lord

Opening Prayer

Reading

Now though the mind is most rapid in its thoughts but the tongue
needs words, and a long recital of intermediary speech. For the eye
embraces at once a multitude of the "starry choir" but when anyone
wishes to describe them one by one, the Morning-star, the Evening-
star, he has need of many words. In like manner again the mind in
the briefest moment compasses earth and sea and all the bounds
of the universe; but what it conceives in an instant, it uses many
words to describe. As forcible as the example I have mentioned is, it
is still after all weak and inadequate. For we do not say all we ought
to about God (for that is known to him only), but only as much as
the capacity of our human nature has received, and only as much as
our weakness can bear. For we do not explain what God is but can-
didly confess that we do not have exact knowledge of him. When it
comes to speaking about God, we must confess that our ignorance
is the best knowledge. Therefore, magnify the Lord with me, and
let us exalt his Name together—all of us in common, for one alone

is powerless; and even if we are all united together, we cannot exalt him as we ought,…even if all the children of the whole Church throughout the world, both that which now is and that which shall be, should meet together, they would not be able worthily to sing the praises of their Shepherd.

CYRIL OF JERUSALEM

ADAPTED FROM *THE CATECHETICAL LECTURES*, VI.2

Meditation

Cyril argues that since all our examples of God and all our speech about him are weak, we must conclude "that our ignorance is the best knowledge." Ignorance is all we have. On the basis of this astonishing claim, he builds an even more astonishing exhortation: We must *confess* that ignorance is our best knowledge, "Therefore, magnify the Lord with me, and let us exalt his Name together."

How do we move from ignorance to exaltation? How do we build praise of God on not knowing God? One answer is that we can know truths about God without knowing every truth there is to know. But even our knowledge of these truths is incomplete. What are we to do? We are to magnify the Lord! And notice how Cyril exhorts us to magnify the Lord: "all of us in common, for one alone is powerless." This is the *via positiva*. Adding on. Building up. Spreading out. But even as he is exhorting us to praise God all together, he admits, "even if we are all united together, we cannot exalt him as we ought."

Back to the *via negativa*. If we are incapable of praising God worthily as a Body, why bother praising him at all? Simply put: We do not praise God for his benefit, but for ours. Even as we lift our voices together to build thunderous praise, we grow as a Body moving toward the Unapproachable.

Do I praise God alone? Or do I seek out other voices singing to God?

Hymn to the Transcendent God

Closing Prayer

Novena *via Positiva*

Although what we know about God and can say about him is wholly imperfect, we are nonetheless compelled to speak about what we know of him, believing and behaving as if our knowledge and language are up to the task of describing an indescribable God.

As loved creatures of a loving God, our language about him is necessarily effusive as we give him thanks and praise. What we know about the Father is revealed to us in the Bible, our study of creation, and in the incarnation of Christ Jesus. And even though our understanding of this single revelation will always be imperfect this side of heaven, we hold that he who has revealed himself is eternally perfect, perfection himself.

This way of talking about God is called *cataphatic* theology or the *via positiva,* "the way of affirmation." Along with deepening their "divine ignorance" by talking about who and what God is not (*via negativa*), biblical writers and early Church theologians struggled to compose affirmative descriptions of the Divine that explained a revealed truth about God. In the historical struggles against state persecution and heretical doctrine, these writers established positive limits for the language and images we use to teach the truth of God's self-revelation.

This novena calls you to take the *via positiva*—to pray along the cataphatic path to deepen your understanding of and devotion to God, he who shows his perfect self to his imperfect creatures.

Opening Prayer

Merciful and gracious Lord, blessed is your holy name above all the stars of heaven! Blessed forever are your works among your people, and holy forever is your name! Your Word is beauty and goodness; divine and eternal are your works; your judgments are unerring and kind. Though we cannot know you as you know yourself, you reveal to us the all we are gifted to know. As we grow in our understanding of your self-revelation, accept our praise and thanksgiving as a spiritual sacrifice worthy of your ears alone. You are with us always. Keep us close to you. In Christ's name we pray. Amen.

Hymn of Praise

> Bless the Lord, O my soul, and all that is within me,
> > bless his holy name.
> Bless the Lord, O my soul, and do not forget all his benefits—
> who forgives all your iniquity, who heals all your diseases
> who redeems your life from the Pit, who crowns you with
> > steadfast love and mercy
> who satisfies you with good as long as you live so that
> > your youth is renewed like the eagle's.
> The Lord works vindication and justice for all who are
> > oppressed.
> He made known his ways to Moses, his acts to the people
> > of Israel.
> The Lord is merciful and gracious,
> > slow to anger and abounding in steadfast love.
> He will not always accuse, nor will he keep his anger forever.

He does not deal with us according to our sins,
nor repay us according to our iniquities.
For as the heavens are high above the earth,
so great is his steadfast love toward those who fear him;
as far as the east is from the west,
so far he removes our transgressions from us.
As a father has compassion for his children,
so the Lord has compassion for those who fear him.
For he knows how we were made;
he remembers that we are dust.
As for mortals, their days are like grass;
they flourish like a flower of the field;
for the wind passes over it, and it is gone,
and its place knows it no more.
But the steadfast love of the Lord is from everlasting to
everlasting, and his righteousness to children's children
Bless the Lord, all his hosts, his ministers that do his will.
Bless the Lord, all his works, in all places of his dominion.
Bless the Lord, O my soul.

ADAPTED FROM PSALM 103

Closing Prayer

Lord God, we name you Goodness, Majesty, Beauty, Truth; we name you Perfect Holiness, Word Made Flesh, Eternal Spirit; we name you Tree of Life, divine love, Essential Light. You are one God—Father, Son, Holy Spirit—one Creator of the universe; one Word of creation; one Spirit re-creating all. We lift our voices to sing of your glory, giving you all gratitude, all adoration, sacrificing body and soul to your holy works. Without you, we are not. Without you ,we are nothing. Lead us to love you more and better. Keep us in your loving care. In Christ's name we pray. Amen.

DAY ONE

We call him love

Daily Opening Prayer

Reading

What do the theologians mean when at one time they call him Love, and Loving-kindness, and at another, Loved and Esteemed?…They call him esteemed and loved, as Beautiful and Good: but again Love and Loving-kindness, as being at once moving and conducting Power to himself—the alone—self Beautiful and Good, by reason of Itself, and being a manifestation of Itself through Itself, and a good Progression of the surpassing union, and a loving Movement, simplex, self-moved, self-operating, pre-existing in the Good, and from the Good bubbling forth to things existing, and again returning to the Good, in which also the divine love indicates distinctly Its own unending and unbeginning, as if it were a sort of everlasting circle whirling round in unerring combination, by reason of the Good, from the Good, and in the Good, and to the Good, and ever advancing and remaining and returning in the same and throughout the same. And these things our illustrious initiator divinely set forth throughout his Hymns of Love.

DIONYSIUS THE AEROPAGITE

THE DIVINE NAMES, 4.16

Meditation

Surely we can say God is good. We can say God is goodness. He is also Truth, Holiness, Beauty, and Being. We too are good, true, and beautiful, and we most certainly have our being; we exist. In the long tradition of our faith, we understand that merely existing is good. Just being here is true and beautiful. Why? Insofar as we exist, we participate in Being himself. We cannot but be good so long as we exist as creatures of a good God.

Since our very being here demonstrates God's love, and charged as we are by our baptismal vows to do his work, we turn a reflective gaze on our being, our being-here-right-now, and ask

In words, thoughts, and deeds, am I living as God's sacrament to the world, an outward sign of his presence, an effective means of his grace for others?

Hymn of Praise

Daily Closing Prayer

DAY TWO

He imparted his glorious splendor

Daily Opening Prayer

Reading

God in his mercy stooped and came down,—to mingle his compassion with the water,—and to blend the nature of his majesty—with the wretched bodies of men—he made occasion by the water—to come down and to dwell in us:—like to the occasion of mercy—when he came down and dwelt in the womb:—O the mercies of God—Who seeks for himself all occasions to dwell in us! To the cave in Horeb he stooped and came down,—and on Moses he caused his majesty to dwell;—he imparted his glorious splendour to mortals.—There was in this a figure of Baptism:—he Who came down and dwelt in it,—tempers within the water—the might of his majesty,—that he may dwell in the feeble.—On Moses dwelt the Breath,—and on you the Perfecting of Christ.

SAINT EPHRAIM THE SYRIAN

ADAPTED FROM *FIFTEEN HYMNS FOR THE FEAST OF THE EPIPHANY,* VIII

Meditation

Even before we are baptized into the Body of Christ, we begin to grow in his perfection. As creatures—created beings—we share in the one Goodness that creates and sustains the universe. With our baptism, our death, and resurrection in the water of life, we step into the great drama of salvation, all those moments in our human history when God "stooped and came down" into his creation, where he "imparted his glorious splendour" and lightened the darkness all around us. All of these moments were instances of God reaching toward us to perfect us, to reshape us into people capable of seeing and hearing more clearly his presence among us.

When and where is God stooping down to reveal his graces, to unveil his gifts? When and where do I see his glorious splendor? In large ways and small, how do I help others see and hear what he has to reveal?

Hymn of Praise

Daily Closing Prayer

DAY THREE

Named Father by the very Word

Daily Opening Prayer

Reading

Now since Deity by its very nature is permanently and immutably the same in all that pertains to its essence, nor did it at any time fail to be anything that it now is, nor will it at any future time be anything that it is not now, and since he Who is the very Father was named Father by the Word, and since in the Father the Son is implied,—since these things are so, we of necessity believe that he Who admits no change or alteration in his nature was always entirely what he is now, or, if there is anything which he was not, that he assuredly is not now. Since then he is named Father by the very Word, he assuredly always was Father, and is and will be even as he was. For surely it is not lawful in speaking of the Divine and unimpaired Essence to deny that what is excellent always belonged to lt. For if he was not always what he now is, he certainly changed either from the better to the worse or from the worse to the better, and of these assertions the impiety is equal either way, whichever statement is made concerning the Divine nature. But in fact the Deity is incapable of change and alteration. So, then, everything that is excellent and good is always contemplated in the fountain of excellency...Well then, it has been demonstrated by these proofs that the Son is from all eternity to be contemplated in the Father, in Whom he is, being Life and Light and Truth, and every noble name and conception—to say that the

Father ever existed by himself apart from these attributes is a piece of the utmost impiety and infatuation.

GREGORY OF NYSSA

AGAINST EUNOMIUS, 2.2

Meditation

It would seem that a god incapable of change—a god wholly unmoved and unmoving—would be unworthy of our trust, much less our worship. Reigning from above as Deity or Essence or Power, such a god would be distant, detached and, if not entirely dispassionate towards its creation, unfriendly. How does Life, Light, and Truth suffer with us? How does Perfection, Excellence, the One intervene in our lives to produce the miraculous, to reveal itself to us? How can we be comforted by Being Itself? This cold, distant deity is not the god we have come to know as the one who died for us.

Why do our early Church Fathers insist on naming the God of history "Essence," "Pure Act," "Source"? If these names do not adequately denote whom we're worshiping, why use them at all? What gain is there in trying to reach for the unreachable? To speak the unspeakable? How do names like "Father" and "Son" differ from names like "Font of Life" and "Creator"?

Hymn of Praise

Daily Closing Prayer

DAY FOUR

One source of peace for all

Daily Opening Prayer

Reading

Come, then, let us extol the Peace Divine, and Source of conciliation, by hymns of peace! For this it is which unifies all, and engenders, and effects the agreement and fellowship of all. Since all things aspire to it, which turns their divided multiplicity into the thorough Oneness, and unifies the tribal war of the whole into a homogeneous dwelling together, by the participation of the divine Peace. With regard, then, to the more reverend of the conciliating powers, these indeed are united to themselves and to each other, and to the one Source of Peace of the whole; and the things that are under them, these they unite also to themselves and to each other, and to the One and all-perfect Source and Cause of the Peace of all, which, passing indivisibly to the whole, limits and terminates and secures everything, as if by a kind of bolts, which bind together things that are separated; and do not permit them, when separated, to rush to infinity and the boundless, and to become without order, and without stability, and destitute of God, and to depart from the union amongst themselves, and to become intermingled in each other, in every sort of confusion.

DIONYSIUS THE AEROPAGITE

THE DIVINE NAMES, 11.1

Meditation

It should not be surprising for us to read that God is the source of our unity and therefore our peace. As we are each bound to him individually, we are also bound to one another through him. This raises a question about the apparently inevitable conflicts that plague human history—war, economic collapse, political upheaval. If God is the "Source and Cause of the peace of all" and binds "together things that are separated" "as if by a kind of bolts," why do we so often find ourselves in violent conflicts with others? Even individually, we experience emotional and physical disruption, seeming to reveal a falsehood at the root of the Christian claim that God is our unity and our peace.

The Church Fathers tended to understanding our unity in metaphysical terms rather than in strictly political terms; that is, they understood God to be the principle of created order, the One Who orders the multiplicity of the cosmos into a viable whole. Dionysius, though not a Church Father himself, writes here that God holds his creation in ordered being so that when we are separated by "tribal war," we do not "rush to infinity and the boundless."

When I find us in conflict, how do I understand God's will that we be united in his peace? How do I understand God's will that we not fall headlong into chaos and confusion?

Hymn of Praise

Daily Closing Prayer

DAY FIVE

Seeking the things that are above

Daily Opening Prayer

Reading

In order, therefore, that the human mind might be purged from falsities...Holy Scripture, which suits itself to babes has not avoided words drawn from any class of things really existing, through which, as by nourishment, our understanding might rise gradually to things divine and transcendent. For, in speaking of God, it has both used words taken from things corporeal, as when it says, "Hide me under the shadow of your wings;" and it has borrowed many things from the spiritual creature in order to signify that which indeed is not so, but needs to be said: for instance, "I the Lord your God am a jealous God;" and, "I repent that I have made man." But Holy Scripture has used no words—either figures of speech or enigmatic sayings—from non-existing things in order to speak of God...For divine Scripture tends to frame allurements for children from the things which are found in the creature so that, according to their ability, the affections of the weak may be moved to seek those things that are above, and to leave those things that are below.

SAINT AUGUSTINE

ADAPTED FROM *ON THE TRINITY,* I.1.2

Meditation

When we were children, we used our fingers to learn to count. Our teachers showed us how to do basic arithmetic using apples, oranges, balls, and pencils. Eventually, we moved on to learn more abstract ways of calculating numerical and geometrical relationships using formulas and equations. If we were especially talented at imagining these relationships, we may have been taught to think in four dimensions using functional variables. Each step we took deeper into abstraction depended on the integrity of all the steps below. Starting with counted fingers, we move to pure numerical systems. These complex systems are radically dependent on our ability to add and subtract.

God's self-revelation works much the same way. In Scripture we have language and images that use the things of the world to point to the divine and the transcendent. As we come to understand God's self-revelation better, we move beyond the "allurements for children" and find the truth in concepts unfettered by concrete allusions.

Do I understand that the people and things I encounter every day are concrete revelations of the Divine? Even though I may have a library of complex images and abstract language to describe the Divine, am I willing to return to the concrete and treat the people and things of creation as signs of God's presence and work?

Hymn of Praise

Daily Closing Prayer

DAY SIX

We come from One

Daily Opening Prayer

Reading

First then let there be laid as a foundation in your soul the doctrine concerning God; that God is One, alone unbegotten, without beginning, change, or variation; neither begotten of another, nor having another to succeed him in his life; who neither began to live in time, nor ever ends: and that he is both good and just; that if ever you hear a heretic say that there is one God who is just and another who is good, you may immediately remember, and discern the poisoned arrow of heresy. For some have impiously dared to divide the One God in their teaching: and some have said that one is the Creator and Lord of the soul, and another of the body; a doctrine at once absurd and impious. For how can a man become the one servant of two masters, when our Lord says in the Gospels, "No man can serve two masters"? There is then One Only God, the Maker both of souls and bodies: One the Creator of heaven and earth, the Maker of Angels and Archangels: many come from the Creator but they come from One, the only Father before all ages—from One only, his Only-begotten Son, our Lord Jesus Christ, by Whom he made "all things visible and invisible."

CYRIL OF JERUSALEM

CATECHETICAL LECTURE, 4.1.4

Meditation

It might seem odd that believers in this postmodern age need to be warned against the age-old temptation of falling into polytheism and idolatry. If we have come to understand God in the highly abstract terms of theology and philosophy, then surely we have abandoned the primitive urge to worship the gods and their earthly totems. Though it is unlikely that believers are tempted to worship statues of Odin or pay homage to trees and rivers as gods, we are still drawn to the glamours of multiplicity, the charms of hedging our bets against divine providence by investing our spiritual wealth in diversified religious portfolios.

The Church's insistence on teaching the oneness of the Divine is more than just a rhetorical move; it's a spiritual truth that stands against what seems to be our tendency to trust in many little gods (money, prestige, power) rather than the One God of revelation.

Reflecting on my spiritual life—both what I say and what I do—could I be justly charged with the sin of polytheism? Where do I invest my trust? My spiritual capital? Who or what do I place on the altar of my heart to worship?

Hymn of Praise

Daily Closing Prayer

DAY SEVEN

Seek higher than creation

Daily Opening Prayer

Reading

"And what is this?" I asked the earth; and it answered, "I am not He;" and all earthly things made the same confession. I asked the sea and the deeps, and the creeping things that lived, and they replied, "We are not your God, seek higher than we." I asked the breezy air, and the universal air with its inhabitants answered, "Anaximenes was deceived, I am not God." I asked the heavens, the sun, moon, and stars: "Neither," say they, "are we the God whom you seek." And I answered to all these things which stand about the door of my flesh, "You have told me concerning my God, that you are not He; tell me something about him." And with a loud voice they exclaimed, "he made us." I questioned them by observing them; and they answered me with their beauty. And then I directed my thoughts to myself, and said, "Who are you?" And I answered, "A man." And in me there is both body and soul, the one without, the other within. With which of these should I seek my God, whom I had sought from earth to heaven through the body—with the lights of my eyes? But the inner part is better; for to it, as both president and judge, all my corporeal messengers gave the answers of heaven and earth, and all the things of heaven and earth said, "We are not God, but he made us." My inner man was made aware of these answers by the ministry of my outer man; I, the inner man, knew all this—I, the soul, through the senses of my body. I asked the vast bulk of the earth of my God, and it answered me, "I am not He, but he made me."

SAINT AUGUSTINE

ADAPTED FROM *CONFESSIONS*, X.6.9

Meditation

It is common for us to think of the relationship between body and soul in terms of a "ghost in a machine." The body contains the soul, or the body is a physical machine that the soul animates. This image often leads us to treat the body with contempt and elevate the soul as the only part of our humanity that matters in the end. The body corrupts, tempts, holds us back. The soul purifies, raises up, clarifies. The problem with this image of the "ghost in a machine" is that it isn't Christian. Who we are as persons is body/soul. God reveals himself to us in Scripture, creation, and Christ Jesus—and to appreciate those requires all of our bodily senses.

Augustine teaches us to look to creation as a sign of God's presence, but we are never to confuse the sign with the thing in itself. Creation is not God. The things of this world—especially the human person, body and soul—point us beyond creation to the Creator.

How do I use my body to grow in holiness? Do I understand creation as a sign of God's presence? Does my "outer person" minister to my "inner person" in a way that pulls me closer to God?

Hymn of Praise

Daily Closing Prayer

DAY EIGHT
I AM THAT I AM

Daily Opening Prayer

Reading

In God we must worship absolute eternity and absolute power. While my mind was dwelling on these and on many like thoughts, I chanced upon the books which, according to the tradition of the Hebrew faith, were written by Moses and the prophets, and found in these words spoken by God the Creator testifying about himself "I AM THAT I AM," and again, "he THAT IS has sent me to you." I confess that I was amazed to find in them a description of God so exact that it expressed in the terms best adapted to human understanding an unattainable insight into the mystery of the Divine nature. For no property of God which the mind can grasp is more characteristic of him than existence, since existence, in the absolute sense, cannot be used to describe that which shall come to an end, nor for that which has had a beginning. He who now joins continuity of being with the possession of perfect happiness could not in the past, nor can in the future, be non-existent; for whatsoever is Divine can neither be originated nor destroyed. Since God's eternity is inseparable from himself, it was worthy of him to reveal this one thing, that he is, as the assurance of his absolute eternity.

HILARY OF POITIERS

ADAPTED FROM *ON THE TRINITY*, 1.4, 5

Meditation

God doesn't exist. God isn't a being, not even a supreme being; he is Being himself. Along the *via positiva* we find any number of divine names that purport to describe God or attempt to assign this or that value to him. Though these names may be objectively true, they aren't absolutely true; that is, God is certainly good, but in no sense can we say goodness exhausts everything God is.

Since we're pleased to offer worship to our Creator, we must necessarily do so as the creatures we are. This means we use words, images, music, and symbols to express our understanding of Being himself—terms that benefit our growth in holiness. God doesn't *need* our praise or our thanks or our prayers. We give thanks and praise, and we pray because doing so immerses us more deeply in the divine nature. The path of affirmation leads us further into the glory of God without coming anywhere near the fullness of that glory. We can never exhaust the imprecision of our prayer.

If it's true that I can never adequately describe God or pray in words that precisely address him, what purpose is there in prayer? Isn't simple silence the better path? Is silence itself a form of address? It seems that talking about God is rather futile—why bother?

Hymn of Praise

Daily Closing Prayer

DAY NINE

That your joy may be complete

Daily Opening Prayer

Reading

We declare to you what was from the beginning, what we have heard, what we have seen with our eyes, what we have looked at and touched with our hands, concerning the word of life—this life was revealed, and we have seen it and testify to it, and declare to you the eternal life that was with the Father and was revealed to us—we declare to you what we have seen and heard so that you also may have fellowship with us; and truly our fellowship is with the Father and with his Son Jesus Christ. We are writing these things so that our joy may be complete.

This is the message we have heard from him and proclaim to you, that God is light and in him there is no darkness at all. If we say that we have fellowship with him while we are walking in darkness, we lie and do not do what is true; but if we walk in the light as he himself is in the light, we have fellowship with one another, and the blood of Jesus his Son cleanses us from all sin.

Beloved, we are God's children now; what we will be has not yet been revealed. What we do know is this: when he is revealed, we will be like him, for we will see him as he is. And all who have this hope in him purify themselves, just as he is pure.

Whoever does not love does not know God, for God is love. God's love was revealed among us in this way: God sent his only Son into the world so that we might live through him.

1 JOHN 1:1–7, 3:2–3, 4:8–9

Meditation

We know who we are now: God's children. What we will become as children of God is not entirely clear. Why? John says what we will become hasn't yet been revealed, but when it is revealed to us we will be like God.

Take as our principle here the idea that an acorn always grows into an oak—never an elm or a birch. If we're children of God now and we'll be like him when what we will become is revealed, then it's safe to say we will be God. What this means exactly is unclear, because what we will become (God) isn't entirely clear either. We know an acorn will become an oak. What will this oak look like? How tall? How strong? How long will it thrive? In the same way, we know we will become God—achieve full union with him as his perfected creatures—but we don't know precisely what this will look like until it happens.

What we do know right now is that God is love for us. And if we are to become Love, we must love as he loves us: freely, creatively, abundantly.

Do I see myself as someone who is living in divine love, growing in love, becoming more and more steeped in the freely given gift of life and the creative impulses of God? Do I hope to become God and thereby make myself pure in his service?

Hymn of Praise

Daily Closing Prayer

Novena *via Sophia*

Sophia is one of the more elusive concepts found in the Judeo-Christian tradition. Often named in Scripture "the spirit of God," wisdom is depicted in such a way that we might come to think that she is a spirit separated from God, almost a divine being unto herself. In fact, gnostic sects during the time of the Early Church often adopted Sophia as a feminine companion for God, sometimes even as his wife.

This isn't how the Church understands God's wisdom. At the beginning of the second chapter of his first letter to the Corinthians, Paul places God's wisdom in direct contradiction to the wisdom of this age, human wisdom. Paul addresses the tendency of the Corinthian Church to fall back into the ways of the Greek philosophers and to blend their worship with practices from imported cults.

For Paul, the difference between God's wisdom and human wisdom seems to be that human wisdom doesn't ground itself squarely in the revealed Word of God found in Scripture and the crucified Christ. The objects, methods, conclusions, and goals of human wisdom aren't always consistent with the proclamation of the Gospel.

True wisdom for the Christian is a combination of knowledge, experience, and faith. Knowledge and experience can make you a competent doctor. Experience and faith can make you a reliable source of practical advice. Knowledge and faith can make you a good teacher. But only the three together can make you wise in the ways of the Lord.

This novena will take you into a deeper appreciation of what it means to be "wise in the Lord" and challenge you to live that wisdom daily.

Daily Opening Prayer

God of wisdom and truth, those who live rightly in your light have no fear of darkness or death. Knowing and loving you with a heart and mind open to your justice, hands ready to do the merciful work of Christ, we stand with the saints of the Church in your redeeming wisdom. Discipline our tongues to speak only *to* you and *about* you so that those who will see and hear may look upon our works and heed our words as signs of your boundless compassion. In Christ's name we pray. Amen.

Daily Closing Prayer

Lord of life, we do not court death nor do we draw ourselves to destruction, yet we are sorely tempted to let injustice thrive. When we neglect the discipline of your holy spirit, we risk becoming students of discord, witnesses to jealousy and error rather than lovers of goodness and truth. Your justice is undying; nurture the seed of goodness you planted in us at our creation and bring us whole and new to you as we do works of mercy you have given us. In Christ's name we pray. Amen.

Hymn to Wisdom

As for the earth, out of it comes bread;
but underneath it is turned up as by fire.
Its stones are the place of sapphires,
and its dust contains gold.
But where shall wisdom be found?
And where is the place of understanding?
Mortals do not know the way to it,
and it is not found in the land of the living.
It cannot be bought for gold,
and silver cannot be weighed out as its price.
Where then does wisdom come from?
And where is the place of understanding?
It is hidden from the eyes of all living,
and concealed from the birds of the air.
God understands the way to it,
and he knows its place.
For he looks to the ends of the earth,
and sees everything under the heavens.
He puts his hand to the flinty rock,
and overturns mountains by the roots.
He cuts out channels in the rocks,
and his eyes see every precious thing.
The sources of the rivers he probes;
hidden things he brings to light.
When he gave to the wind its weight,
and apportioned out the waters by measure;
when he made a decree for the rain,

and a way for the thunderbolt;
then he saw it and declared it;
he established it, and searched it out.
And he said to humankind,
Truly, the fear of the Lord, that is wisdom;
and to depart from evil is understanding.

ADAPTED FROM JOB 28

DAY ONE

Wisdom is a kindly spirit

Daily Opening Prayer

Reading

Love righteousness, you rulers of the earth, think of the Lord in goodness and seek him with sincerity of heart; because he is found by those who do not put him to the test, and manifests himself to those who do not distrust him. For perverse thoughts separate people from God, and when his power is tested, it exposes the foolish; because wisdom will not enter a deceitful soul, or dwell in a body enslaved to sin. For a holy and disciplined spirit will flee from deceit, and will leave foolish thoughts behind, and will be ashamed at the approach of unrighteousness. For wisdom is a kindly spirit, but will not free blasphemers from the guilt of their words; because God is witness of their inmost feelings, and a true observer of their hearts, and a hearer of their tongues. Because the spirit of the Lord has filled the world, and that which holds all things together knows what is said…because a jealous ear hears all things, and the sound of grumbling does not go unheard. Beware then of useless grumbling, and keep your tongue from slander; because no secret word is without result, and a lying mouth destroys the soul. Do not invite death by the error of your life, or bring on destruction by the works of your hands; because God did not make death, and he does not delight in the death of the living. For he created all things so that they might exist; the generative forces of the world are wholesome, and there is no destructive poison in them, and the dominion of Hades is not on earth. For righteousness is immortal.

ADAPTED FROM WISDOM 1:1–15

Meditation

We tend to believe a person is sincere in his convictions when his words are made manifest in action. Heart, mind, hands come together to drive a belief into the real world of behavior and result. If the belief being made manifest is evil, then the acts and results will be evil as well. However, the godly person—living righteously in God's will—loves his justice, seeks out his truth, and does his work. We call this person wise.

In what ways am I tempted to believe in God's justice but refrain from doing it? Do I call the work I do in God's name "just" and yet fail to live righteously according to his will?

Hymn to Wisdom

Daily Closing Prayer

DAY TWO

Proven in a furnace

Daily Opening Prayer

Reading

But the souls of the righteous are in the hand of God, and no torment will ever touch them. In the eyes of the foolish they seemed to have died, and their departure was thought to be a disaster, and their going from us to be their destruction; but they are at peace. For though in the sight of others they were punished, their hope is full of immortality. Having been disciplined a little, they will receive great good, because God tested them and found them worthy of himself; like gold in the furnace he tried them, and like a sacrificial burnt-offering he accepted them. In the time of their visitation they will shine forth, and will run like sparks through the stubble. They will govern nations and rule over peoples, and the Lord will reign over them for ever. Those who trust in him will understand truth, and the faithful will abide with him in love, because grace and mercy are upon his holy ones, and he watches over his elect. But the ungodly will be punished as their reasoning deserves, those who disregarded the righteous and rebelled against the Lord; for those who despise wisdom and instruction are miserable. Their hope is vain, their labours are unprofitable, and their works are useless.

WISDOM 3:1–11

Meditation

Living in God's wisdom brings peace. Refusing God's wisdom—neglecting his justice—brings doom. It's not enough for the just to simply possess God's wisdom; that is, knowing the *content* of wisdom is insufficient for living wisely, justly. Wisdom must be understood as an expression of God's truth and lived with radical love, trusting all the while in the divine gifts of grace and mercy.

If we see God's wisdom as nothing more than a deposit of knowledge, an esoteric database of secret information to be known for the sake of knowing, then the entire purpose of wisdom is lost to us. God's wisdom is wise for us only when it lives in us as his justice—the truth done for ourselves and others. Those who live in justice will be tested by the foolish, and they will shine even as they are punished.

Am I courageous enough to live justly in God's wisdom? Am I prepared to be punished for doing so?

Hymn to Wisdom

Daily Closing Prayer

DAY THREE

The desire for wisdom leads to God

Daily Opening Prayer

Reading

For they will be made holy who observe holy things in holiness, and those who have been taught them will find a defence. Therefore set your desire on my words; long for them, and you will be instructed.

Wisdom is radiant and unfading, and she is easily discerned by those who love her, and is found by those who seek her. She hastens to make herself known to those who desire her. One who rises early to seek her will have no difficulty, for she will be found sitting at the gate. To fix one's thought on her is perfect understanding, and one who is vigilant on her account will soon be free from care, because she goes about seeking those worthy of her, and she graciously appears to them in their paths, and meets them in every thought.

The beginning of wisdom is the most sincere desire for instruction, and concern for instruction is love of her, and love of her is the keeping of her laws, and giving heed to her laws is assurance of immortality, and immortality brings one near to God; so the desire for wisdom leads to a kingdom.

Therefore if you delight in thrones and sceptres, O monarchs over the peoples, honor wisdom, so that you may reign for ever.

WISDOM 6:10–21

Meditation

Pope Benedict XVI has noted that our faith can be understood as a kind of erotic theology; that is, we can express our trust in God as our response to his divine seduction. Once seduced, once drawn into the drama of divine love, we desire more and more a deeper and deeper friendship with God. Notice here that God's wisdom is "discerned by those who love her, and is found by those who seek her." First, we must acknowledge that wisdom is lovable, desirable; we must want God's wisdom to comprehend her to our full capacity. Then, desiring wisdom, we seek her out.

But notice as well that wisdom "she goes about seeking those worthy of her, and she graciously appears to them in their paths, and meets them in every thought." God's wisdom is not a passive spirit or a collected set of static propositions. She is a roving spirit hunting for worthy lovers. How do we make ourselves obvious targets for wisdom's seduction? "Therefore set your desire on my words; long for them, and you will be instructed."

Am I vigilant for wisdom, desiring God's words to order my life? If not, what stands between me and God that dampens my desire for his wisdom?

Hymn to Wisdom

Daily Closing Prayer

DAY FOUR

The beginning of wisdom

Daily Opening Prayer

Reading

Praise the Lord!
I will give thanks to the Lord with my whole heart,
in the company of the upright, in the congregation.
Great are the works of the Lord,
studied by all who delight in them.
Full of honour and majesty is his work,
and his righteousness endures for ever.
He has gained renown by his wonderful deeds;
the Lord is gracious and merciful.
He provides food for those who fear him;
he is ever mindful of his covenant.
He has shown his people the power of his works,
in giving them the heritage of the nations.
The works of his hands are faithful and just;
all his precepts are trustworthy.
They are established for ever and ever,
to be performed with faithfulness and uprightness.
He sent redemption to his people;
he has commanded his covenant for ever.
Holy and awesome is his name.

The fear of the Lord is the beginning of wisdom;
all those who practise it have a good understanding.
His praise endures for ever.

PSALM 111

Meditation

It is often noted these days that "fear" in this context is more akin to what we call "awe" than to what we call "horror" or "dread." True, but we cannot move so far away from true fear of the Lord that we forget how utterly other-than the Lord is to his creatures. Incapable of comprehending the full majesty of the Lord as we are, fear seems the perfect response. However, to live always in horror and dread of the Lord is spiritually damaging.

If we can use that fear to measure our imperfection against his perfection and realize that heeding his words is the smart thing to do, we can hear wisdom speak to us. When we open ourselves to God's wisdom, we realize his works are always reliable. And precisely because he is immeasurably more than we are now, we can trust his promises to us. As we grow in righteousness, fear turns to awe and awe to love; in love, wisdom becomes startlingly clear.

In what ways do I resist hearing God's wisdom? How do I put off listening to his words? What do I gain and lose by heeding his wisdom with loyalty and care?

Hymn to Wisdom

Daily Closing Prayer

DAY FIVE

We speak God's wisdom

Daily Opening Prayer

Reading

When I came to you, brothers and sisters, I did not come proclaiming the mystery of God to you in lofty words or wisdom. For I decided to know nothing among you except Jesus Christ, and him crucified. And I came to you in weakness and in fear and in much trembling. My speech and my proclamation were not with plausible words of wisdom, but with a demonstration of the Spirit and of power, so that your faith might rest not on human wisdom but on the power of God.

Yet among the mature we do speak wisdom, though it is not a wisdom of this age or of the rulers of this age, who are doomed to perish. But we speak God's wisdom, secret and hidden, which God decreed before the ages for our glory. None of the rulers of this age understood this; for if they had, they would not have crucified the Lord of glory. But, as it is written, "What no eye has seen, nor ear heard, nor the human heart conceived, what God has prepared for those who love him"—these things God has revealed to us through the Spirit; for the Spirit searches everything, even the depths of God. For what human being knows what is truly human except the human spirit that is within? So also no one comprehends what is truly God's except the Spirit of God. Now we have received not the spirit of the world, but the Spirit that is from God, so that we may understand the gifts bestowed on us by God. And we speak of these things in words not taught by human wisdom but taught by the Spirit, interpreting spiritual things to those who are spiritual.

1 CORINTHIANS 2:1–13

Meditation

Paul writes to the Corinthian Church and takes careful note of how he chooses to speak to them. He explicitly states that he will not speak to them using worldly wisdom, the wisdom of the age.

What Paul is doing here is drawing attention to the difference between the kind of philosophical wisdom the Corinthians are used to hearing in the markets from the wisdom that flows from the power of God. In our materialist-scientific culture, we are accustomed to having God's wisdom challenged by the wisdom of the world. How often do we hear basic Church teachings dismissed as superstition or fairy tales because they cannot stand up under the scrutiny of this age's philosophical analysis? Paul is not instructing us to ignore the goods of science or secular philosophy. Rather, he is telling us to start with God's wisdom, take the good where we find it, leave the world behind, and continue on preaching the good news.

Ultimately, as Christians, our end is not in this world, so even though the wisdom of the world may give us nifty technological gadgets, medical cures, rapid transportation, and enormously efficient production, none of these grant us the divine love we long for and need.

In what ways do I concede God's wisdom to the wisdom of the world? How do I allow the values and priorities of this age to overshadow my commitment to growing in righteousness before the Lord? Do I reject the goods available to me in the world simply because they are produced by the world?

Hymn to Wisdom

Daily Closing Prayer

DAY SIX

The manifold wisdom of God

Daily Opening Prayer

Reading

Those who are wise in mind have a certain attribute of nature peculiar to themselves; and they who have shown themselves capable, receive from the Supreme Wisdom a spirit of perception in double measure. For those who practice the common arts, are highly gifted in what pertains to the senses: in hearing, he who is commonly called a musician; in touch, he who moulds clay; in voice the singer, in smell the perfumer, in sight the engraver of devices on seals. Those also who are occupied in instruction, train the sensibility according to which the poets are susceptible to the influence of measure; the sophists apprehend expression; the logicians, syllogisms; and the philosophers are capable of the contemplation of which themselves are the objects. For sensibility finds and invents; since it persuasively exhorts to application. And practice will increase the application which has knowledge for its end. With reason, therefore, the apostle has called the wisdom of God "manifold," and which has manifested its power "in many departments and in many modes"—by art, by knowledge, by faith, by prophecy—for our benefit. "For all wisdom is from the Lord, and is with him for ever," as says the wisdom of Jesus.

CLEMENT OF ALEXANDRIA

ADAPTED FROM *THE STROMATA*, I.4

Meditation

God's single spirit of wisdom is comprehended in many wisdoms among his creatures. There is divine wisdom in science, medicine, technology, art, literature, and philosophy. To the degree that any of these research and teach the truth, they teach divine truth. There is only one Truth, but there are many expressions of Truth.

Thomas Aquinas teaches us that there can be no contradiction between faith and reason because both have the same source: God. All truth is God's truth. Both faith and reason are divine gifts that manifest the wisdom that seduces us to love God and one another. If God reveals himself in his creation, then a studious application of the gift of reason to that creation must necessarily be a reasoned investigation into God's self-revelation.

However, worldly wisdoms fail when they take what is merely sensible as the fullness of truth and refuse to acknowledge that the things of creation they study have a divine purpose. This is why true wisdom is not just a matter of combining knowledge and experience. Faith must balance the equation; otherwise, we have permanently attached ourselves to impermanence.

Am I able to discern God's manifold wisdom working in the fields of human endeavor? Am I able to distinguish rightly between what is truly wise and merely smart? Am I open to the possibility that God might reveal his truth to me through science, technology, the liberal arts?

Hymn to Wisdom

Daily Closing Prayer

DAY SEVEN

A life worthy of praise

Daily Opening Prayer

Reading

The first wisdom is a life worthy of praise, and kept pure for God, or being purified for him Who is all-pure and all-luminous, Who demands of us, us his only sacrifice, purification—that is, a contrite heart and the sacrifice of praise, and a new creation in Christ, and the new man....The first wisdom is to despise that wisdom which consists of language and figures of speech, and spurious and un-necessary embellishments. Be it mine to speak five words with my understanding in the church, rather than ten thousand words in a tongue, and with the unmeaning voice of a trumpet, which does not rouse my soldier to the spiritual combat. This is the wisdom which I praise.... By this the ignoble have won renown, and the despised have attained the highest honours. By this a crew of fishermen have taken the whole world in the meshes of the Gospel-net, and overcome by a word finished and cut short the wisdom that comes to naught. I count not wise the man who is clever in words, nor him who is of a ready tongue, but unstable and undisciplined in soul, like the tombs which, fair and beautiful as they are outwardly, are fetid with corpses within, and full of manifold ill-savours; but him who speaks but little of virtue, yet gives many examples of it in his practice, and proves the trustworthiness of his language by his life.

SAINT GREGORY NAZIANZEN

ORATION 16.2

Meditation

Gregory gets to the heart of living wisely: fewer flowery statements of faith, more virtuous living. Contrasting the "ignoble [who] have won renown" using sophistry and the "crew of fishermen [who] have taken the whole world in the meshes of the Gospel-net," Gregory sets up for us a clear distinction between the dangerous rhetoric of the man who is "unstable and undisciplined in soul" and the man who "gives many examples [of virtue] in his practice."

The first wise move we can make is to live a life worthy of praise. Though Gregory argues his point in the context of attacking the verbiage of the worldly philosophers, his basic premise is applicable to us all: *talking ain't walking.* Walk the talk, or don't talk the walk. Or perhaps even better: The best way to talk about wisdom is to show yourself living wisely.

When witnessing my faith to others, do I use the "unmeaning voice of a trumpet," or do I give "many examples of it in [my] practice"? Do I find it difficult to live wisely? Do I find myself not living a virtuous life? What is lacking in my prayer life that makes this temptation so difficult to resist?

Hymn to Wisdom

Daily Closing Prayer

DAY EIGHT

Goodness gives birth to itself

Daily Opening Prayer

Reading

First of all we ought to know that a wise man and wisdom, a truthful man and truth, a just man and justice, a good man and goodness, have a mutual relationship, and depend on one another, in this way. Goodness is not created, not made, not born; rather it is what gives birth and bears the good man; and the good man, insofar as he is good is unmade and uncreated, and yet he is born, the child and the son of goodness. In the good man goodness gives birth to itself and to everything that is. Being, knowing, loving, working—goodness pours all this into the good man, and the good man accepts all his being, knowing, loving and working from the innermost heart of goodness, and from it alone. That which is good and goodness are nothing else than one single goodness in everything, apart from the one bearing and the other being born; but the goodness does bear and that it is born in the good man, this is all one thing, one life. Everything the good man has, he receives both from goodness and also in goodness. That is where he is and lives and dwells. That is where he knows himself and everything that he knows, and loves everything that he loves, and he works with goodness in goodness, and goodness with him and in him works all its works.

MEISTER ECKHART

THE BOOK OF DIVINE CONSOLATION 1

IN COLLEDGE AND MCGINN, 209–10

Meditation

When we do good works, we do so as a matter of participating in Goodness; that is, we do good because we are embraced by Goodness himself. It follows then that when we are wise, true, just, beautiful, we are all these because we participate in he who is wisdom, truth, justice, and beauty.

Eckhart argues that Goodness is not made or born, but rather expressed in the birth and life of the good person. We know ourselves and others most intimately when we participate in the knowledge and love God provides. We love, live, and work best when we delve into the breadth and depth of God who is love and life.

Why this insistence on locating our goodness and wisdom in the Goodness and Wisdom that is God? This is at once an acknowledgment of our divine origins and our human limitations, our beginnings from nothing and our flourishing in everything that is to the boundaries of created capacity. It's also an expression of hope in our promised future. Insofar as we work alongside God—live and move and have our being in him—we become him in the end.

How do I express God's wisdom to others? Am I sufficiently aware enough of my limitations as a creature to admit that I need God to be myself most fully?

Hymn to Wisdom

Daily Closing Prayer

DAY NINE

Who among you is wise?

Daily Opening Prayer

Reading

So also the tongue is a small member, yet it boasts of great exploits. How great a forest is set ablaze by a small fire! And the tongue is a fire. The tongue is placed among our members as a world of iniquity; it stains the whole body, sets on fire the cycle of nature, and is itself set on fire by hell. For every species of beast and bird, of reptile and sea creature, can be tamed and has been tamed by the human species, but no one can tame the tongue—a restless evil, full of deadly poison. With it we bless the Lord and Father, and with it we curse those who are made in the likeness of God. From the same mouth come blessing and cursing. My brothers and sisters, this ought not to be so. Does a spring pour forth from the same opening both fresh and brackish water? Can a fig tree, my brothers and sisters, yield olives, or a grapevine figs? No more can salt water yield fresh.

Who is wise and understanding among you? Show by your good life that your works are done with gentleness born of wisdom. But if you have bitter envy and selfish ambition in your hearts, do not be boastful and false to the truth. Such wisdom does not come down from above, but is earthly, unspiritual, devilish. For where there is envy and selfish ambition, there will also be disorder and wickedness of every kind. But the wisdom from above is first pure, then peaceable, gentle, willing to yield, full of mercy and good fruits, without a trace of partiality or hypocrisy. And a harvest of righteousness is sown in peace for those who make peace.

JAMES 3:5–18

Meditation

Against the Pharisees, Jesus argued that it's not what goes into our stomachs, but what comes out of our mouths that can betray us to be corrupted. It's no easy thing to tame the human tongue. It's quite easy to see, however, that a spring cannot give both fresh and polluted water at the same time. The source of the spring is either pure or poisoned, and we know the condition of the source by its output.

How can the source of one's poisoned speech be purified? Again, no simple solution surfaces, but James notes that living a good life that shows the works of wisdom and understanding is the first step.

Bitter jealousy and self-ambition have no place in the life lived wisely. Envying the gifts of others and seeking self-promotion at the expense of others is "earthly, unspiritual, devilish." It follows then that a life lived in wisdom will be heavenly, spiritual, angelic. Such a life imitates its source and shows itself to be "peaceable, gentle, willing to yield, full of mercy and good fruits."

If my heart is bitter, can I produce sweet words? If my heart is sweet, why do I produce bitter words? What power do I give my tongue in disputes, agreements, meditations? Do others see me as a source of wisdom?

Hymn to Wisdom

Daily Closing Prayer

Part Three
The Litanies

Litany of the Holy Spirit

Divine heart, one true God — **Hear us as we pray.**

Spirit of truth and insight — **Show us the Way and the Life.**

Spirit of devotion and integrity — **Give us awe and wonder.**

Spirit of kindness and comfort — **Show us mercy and care.**

Spirit of worship and delight — **Bring us to our knees in adoration.**

Spirit of peace and patience — **Grant us serenity and endurance.**

Spirit of obedience and meekness — **Help us listen with humility.**

Spirit of benevolence and goodness — **Give us generosity.**

Generous love of the Father for the Son — **Engrave your presence on our hearts.**

Abundant love of the Son for the Father — **Shine through our deeds.**

Living water of our baptism — **Free us from all our sins.**

From all the devil's works — **Free us, O Holy Spirit.**

From all uncleanliness of body and spirit

From all excess and material greed

From all inordinate attachments

From all hypocrisy and deception

From all imperfections and bad habits

From our own weak wills

From disparaging tongues

From gossip and insult
From our disordered passions and appetites
From our ignorance of your holy inspirations
From our hatred of duty and obligation
From love of comfort and luxury
From the idols of money, power, and prestige
From anyone who leads us away from you

Loving Father   **Forgive us.**
Redeeming Word   **Save us.**
Re-creating Spirit   **Enlighten us.**

Lamb of God, you take away the sins of the world
                      **Send us your divine
                      consolation.**
Lamb of God, you take away the sins of the world
                      **Fill us with the gifts of your
                      Spirit.**
Lamb of God, you take away the sins of the world
                      **Multiply in us the fruits of the
                      Spirit.**

Come, O Holy Spirit	**And fill the hearts of your faithful.**
Enkindle in us the fire of your love	**And give us a new heaven and earth.**
Send forth your divine Spirit	**And we will be re-created in Christ.**
Renew the face of your creation	**And we give you thanks and praise.**

Let us pray: O Blessed Lord, by the fire of divine love you teach your faithful to be Christ for one another. Give us the Holy Spirit of wisdom and peace that we may always know and understand the right use of your self-revelation to us. We rejoice in your comfort and care, looking toward our life of Beauty with you in heaven. Bring to fruition and harvest the seeds of holiness you have planted in us. We ask this as we ask all things, in the powerful name of Christ Jesus, our Lord. Amen.

Litany of the Holy Name of Jesus

Blessed be the holy name of Jesus among the stars of heaven!
Amen.
Blessed be the holy name of Jesus among the creatures
of the earth!
Blessed be the holy name of Jesus always and forever!

Prayer of Saint John Vianney

(if in a group, recite together)

I love you, my God, and my only desire is to love you until the last breath of my life.

I love you, O my infinitely lovable God, and I would rather die loving you than live without loving you.

I love you, Lord; the only grace I ask is to love you eternally.

My God, if my tongue cannot say in every moment that I love you, I want my heart to repeat it to you as often as I draw breath.

The Litany

Jesus, splendor of the blessed trinity, brightness of eternal light

Jesus, Word made flesh, Father of the world to come, mighty God

Jesus, star of justice, Son of blessed Mary, joy of the angels

Jesus, God of peace, author of life, good shepherd

Jesus, most powerful, most kind, most admirable

Jesus, most patient, most obedient, meek and humble of heart

Jesus, lover of chastity, lover of us all, model of virtue

Jesus, zealous lover of souls, our refuge, father of the poor

Jesus, treasure of the faithful, home for sinners

Jesus, true light, eternal wisdom, ineffable beauty

Jesus, infinite goodness, our Truth, our Way, and our Life

Jesus, king of the patriarchs, master of the apostles

Jesus, teacher of the evangelists, strength of the martyrs

Jesus, light of confessors, purity of virgins, crown of saints

Jesus, high priest, holy prophet, and preacher

Jesus, abandoned, betrayed, and beaten

Jesus, crucified, resurrected, and ascended

Jesus, I AM HE WHO IS.

From your wrath **Spare me.**

From the traps of the devil and his dark angels

Protect me.

From the spirits of anger, greed, avarice, pride, envy, sloth, and lust

Protect me.

From sin and everlasting death **Protect me.**

From the neglect of your inspirations

Protect me.

By the mystery of your Incarnation	**You show me my purpose.**
By your birth	**You make me a son of the father.**
By your nativity	**You teach me to have the faith of a child.**
By your most divine life	**You make me your disciple and prophet.**
By your most holy Eucharist	**You share your body and blood.**
By your agony and passion	**You teach me how to suffer well.**
By your cross and dereliction	**You make me a priest and a sacrifice.**
By your death and burial	**You show me I too will die.**
By your crucifixion	**You teach me to die for my friends.**
By your resurrection	**You give me eternal life with you.**
By your ascension	**You bring me to your throne.**
By your joys	**You give me your joy and your peace.**
By your glory	**You share with me your divine nature.**

Lamb of god, you take away the sins of the world
Have mercy on me.
Lamb of god, you take away the sins of the world
Have mercy on me.
Lamb of god, you take away the sins of the world
Bring me your peace.

O Lord Jesus Christ, you have said, "Ask, and it will be given you; search, and you will find; knock, and the door will be opened for you." Give to me the gift of your divine love that I may ever love you with my whole heart, in word and deed, and never cease praising you.

Closing Prayer

O merciful Jesus, in your infancy you began your ministry as prophet and priest. You became my Savior by shedding your precious blood for me, assuming for all that name above all names; I thank you for these revelations of your infinite love. I venerate your sacred name with Gabriel, the angel who named you, *Emmanuel,* and I unite my affections to the tender love the name *Jesus* has inflamed in the hearts of your saints.

Animated with a firm faith in your unerring word and strengthened with confidence in your mercy, I humbly remind you of the promise you made: That where two or three assemble in your name, you would be in the midst of them. Jesus, come to me and the company of your saints and angels, for it is in your sacred name that I am here; come into my heart that I may be ruled by your holy spirit; in your mercy give to me, through your most holy name, which is the joy of heaven, the terror of hell, the consolation of the suffering, and the solid ground of my unshakable confidence, all my holy needs.

Blessed Mother of our Redeemer, you suffer with your Son as he sheds his sacred blood and assumes for me the name of *Jesus.* Obtain for me through his most holy name all my holy needs and the needs of those for whom I pray: [*names*].

Pray, Blessed Mother, that your son's passionate love may imprint his sacred name on my heart, that his name may always be in my mind and always on my lips; that his name may defend me from despair and be my refuge from all the temptations and trials of this life; and in the hour of my death, may his name be my consolation and support. Amen.

Blessed be the most holy name of Jesus among
    the stars of heaven   **Amen.**
Blessed be the most holy name of Jesus among the
    creatures of the earth
Blessed be the most holy name of Jesus always and forever

Litania creationis ex nihilio

How did the universe begin? Why is there something rather than nothing? Ancient philosophers, biblical prophets, the Church Fathers, medieval philosophers and theologians, and scientists have tackled these questions for centuries.

From our Tradition, rooted in biblical witness and developed for over 2,000 years, the Church has consistently taught that the universe is a free creation of divine love accomplished through *creatio ex nihilio*; that is, God freely created the universe—everything that is—out of nothing.

Nothing here must be understood in its absolute sense, "no-thing-ness," from "no thing" was the universe created, from nothing preexisting in space or time. The universe—all created things—are contingent beings relying entirely on Being himself for their origin, their continuing existence, and their end.

Acknowledging our radical dependence on God is the first step in cultivating the humility proper to our growth in holiness. This litany focuses us on the gift of our creation.

All the stars of heaven, give thanks and praise

Bless the Lord forever!

All the creatures of the earth, give thanks and praise
All that swim under the waters, give thanks and praise

Opening Prayer

Let us pray: Father Creator, speaking the Word of divine love over the Void, you draw from nothing everything that is; at your Word creation bursts into being, and from that Word everything that is draws its beginning, its being, and its purpose. In you we live, we move, we have our being, and with you, we have our end. With hearts and minds turned to your creation, we give you thanks and praise for the love you reveal to us in all the creatures of this world, and we ask that you bless us with your abundant mercy and care. In the name of Christ Jesus, the Word of divine love, we pray. Amen.

Praise the Father, creator of all that is

Praise him and bless him!

Praise the Son, redeeming wisdom

Praise the Holy Spirit, re-creating love

All creatures with voices raised high, praise him

We praise him!

All creatures with voices raised high, bless him

We bless him!

All creatures with voices raised high, give him thanks

We give him thanks!

All saints in heaven
All martyrs and virgins
All angels and archangels
All elders of the altar
All rulers of the earth
All judges of the nations
All peoples of every tongue
All tribes on every continent
All countries of the world
All saints among us
All mothers and fathers
All sons and daughters
All children

Praise him and bless him!

Give praise, sun and moon
Give praise, stars and clouds
Give praise, birds of the air
Give praise, creatures of the seas
Give praise, creatures of the forests
Give praise, hills and valleys
Give praise, mountains and rivers
Give praise, darkness and light
Give praise, trees and grasslands
Give praise, summers and springs
Give praise, winters and autumns
Give praise in every tongue

Give thanks and praise!

Father, from nothing you made us   **We give you thanks!**
Father, from void you us drew out
Father, with a Word you gave us life
Father, in your love, we live and move
Father, in you we have our being

For the blessings of this life,
For the gift of life,
For the gift of eternal life.
(*pause for silent prayer*)

Credo

Leader: With humility, we reaffirm our faith in God the Father of us all:

Together: I believe our God breathed the Word of divine love over the void, and the universe was created. For my creation, I give him thanks and praise. I believe our God breathes the Word of divine love over his creation, and we are redeemed. For my re-creation, I give him thanks and praise. I believe our God will breathe the Word of divine love at our end, and we will be given new life with him in heaven. For my life eternal, I give him thanks and praise.

Concluding Prayer

Let us pray: Father, we give you thanks and praise for all you have given us in your creation. Place in our hearts and minds a love for your creation equal to your own so we might be better stewards of all you have given us. Help us grow in humility as we live and move and have our being in this wondrous universe you created. Knowing how much you love us and care for us, we know you will never abandon us to the void. And so, as creatures dependent on your very Word for our being, we receive from you all the blessings you will for us. With love you made us, with love you sustain us, and with love you will bring us home to you. We ask all this, as we ask all things, in the name of Christ Jesus, your Word of divine love. Amen.

Litany of Faith
in the Holy Trinity

This litany of faith is an adaptation of *A Declaration of Faith*, written by Gregory the Wonderworker (circa 265). This declaration on the holy trinity was composed almost a century before the Nicene Creed and reflects a thoroughly orthodox understanding of the trinity. Gregory professes his faith in a triune God—three persons, one God, distinct but inseparable.

Opening Prayer

Holy and Eternal God, giver of all that is, this day we profess our trust in your fatherly care, holding ourselves to the baptismal promises that make us your adopted children, your heirs, and your Church. By this profession, we commit ourselves once again to the unflinching and unerring proclamation of your Gospel.

Leader: By the urging of the Holy Spirit and in his presence, we pray:

There is one God, the Father of the living Word
                              We place our trust in you.
Who is his abiding wisdom and power
Eternal Image, perfect begetter of the perfect begotten
Father of the only begotten Son, Jesus Christ.

There is one Lord, only of the only, God of God
Image and likeness of the divine, creating Word
perfect wisdom, the foundation of all things,
divine power shaping the whole of creation
true Son of true Father, invisible of invisible
incorruptible of incorruptible, one Being,
immortal of immortal, eternal of eternal.
And there is one Holy Spirit, having his life from God
being made manifest to us by the Son
image of the Son, perfect image of the perfect;
life himself, the cause of the living; holy fount,
sanctity himself, the giver of holiness;
Christ, in whom is manifested God the Father
he who is above all and in all,
God the Son, who is through all.
There is a perfect trinity undivided,
one in glory, eternity, and sovereignty.
There is nothing created in the trinity.
Neither was the Son ever wanting to the Father
nor the Spirit to the Son.
Without variation, without change
the same trinity abides forever.

Holy trinity, one Lord, forgive our sins.

Lord, have mercy.

Holy trinity, one Word, forgive our sins.
Holy trinity, one Spirit, forgive our sins.

Closing Prayer

Holy God, foundation of all things, we have professed our faith in you. Trusting now in the life to come, we rededicate ourselves to the pursuit of perfection by following the path of holiness first walked by your Son. Serving as he served, preaching as he preached, we lay all our hopes at the feet of the one servant who never fails, Christ Jesus. Give us the strength and determination to set aside all that distracts us from the works of compassion you have set before us. Set us free in love that we may love as you first loved us. We ask this in Jesus' holy name. **Amen.**

In the Name of the Father, who speaks the Word (+)   **Amen.**
In the Name of the Son, who is the Word (+)
In the Name of the Holy Spirit, who is the Word, we speak (+)

Litany of Theosis

In his monumental work, *Summa theologiae,* Saint Thomas Aquinas writes, "The only-begotten Son of God, wanting to make us sharers in his divinity, assumed our nature, so that he, made man, might make men gods." Though this may sound vaguely paganistic, it is in fact Saint Thomas's way of teaching us how we are saved as fallen human beings. Pulling on the Platonic notion of "participation," Thomas expands on the biblical idea that we "live, move, and have our being" in the perfect Being who is God.

Original sin scarred all human existence with disobedience, leaving us, even now, broke and incapable on our own of reaching the perfection we were made to enjoy. God the Father sent his only begotten Son to become a man like one of us in all things but sin so we might become, like him, human and divine.

As Peter writes in his second letter, "His divine power has given us everything needed for life and godliness,...through them you may escape from the corruption that is in the world because of lust, and may become participants of the divine nature" (2 Peter 1:3–4).

Theosis is one way to describe how we come to share in the life of the divine trinity: We become God, participating in his glory as perfected human creatures, redeemed in the sacrifice of the God-Man, Christ Jesus. We are fully possessed by God, though we can never fully possess him. Though we can never know God as he knows himself, we can know him fully as he reveals himself to us in his immanent action in creation.

Opening Prayer

Let us pray: Father, you grant us life and godliness and bring us to your perfection through the sacrifice of your only Son on the cross. Just as he emptied himself and became human like one of us, we too desire for nothing more than to empty ourselves of disordered passions and strive, with the help of your grace, to become like Christ for others. As we progress toward our place at your side in heaven, give us all we need to cooperate with your re-creating acts in us and among us. You show us the Way, the Truth, and the Life. Help us better live, move, and have our being in you. In the name of the one whom we strive to become, Christ Jesus, we pray. Amen.

The Litany

God the Father is our Way

In him we live, we move, we have our being.

God the Son is our Truth
God the Holy Spirit is our Life

Christ who is Son of God by nature **Made us children of God by grace.**

Christ who is fully human
Christ who is fully divine
Christ who is emptied
Christ who is a slave like one of us
Christ who is born as man
Christ who is humble
Christ who is obedient to death
Christ who is killed on a cross

Christ who is highly exalted
Christ whose name is above all names
Christ at whose name every knee bends
Christ whose name every tongue confesses
Christ who is Lord, the glory of God the Father

God, divine love, gives us all things **For our life and our holiness.**
God, divine love, calls us to know him
God, divine love, calls us to his glory
God, divine love, calls us to his excellence
God, divine love, gives us every promise
God, divine love, releases us from corruption
God, divine love, shares with us his divine life

In baptism and anointing with the Spirit   **We are partakers in the divine life.**

In the Eucharist and reconciliation
In chastity and obedience
In the Body of Christ, the Church
In feeding the hungry
In visiting the sick
In clothing the naked
In welcoming the stranger
In loving our neighbor
In loving ourselves
In loving our God
In preaching his Good News
In teaching his truth

In witnessing to his mercy
In testifying for his hope
In rejoicing for his love
In becoming Christ for others

As partakers in the divine life **We grow in holiness.**
As sharers of the ministry of Christ
As participants in the Incarnation
As players in the Father's plan
As members of his body
As followers along his Way
As listeners of his Truth
As citizens of his Life

When we grow in holiness **We become Christ.**
When we faithfully pray
When we proclaim his mercy
When we witness to his ministry
When we are zealous for souls
When we care for the neglected
When we listen and do his will
When we take up our cross
When we suffer for his name's sake
When we die for our friends
When we become Christ **We die for the salvation of the world.**

Let us pray: Lord, you sent your Son to take the form of a slave, to humble himself in becoming one of us, to suffer and die for us, give us the habits of trust and good will so that we too may find our way to the crosses we have been given. Grant us the strength to lift and carry those crosses for his sake, so that we may approach you on the Last Day knowing we have done all we could with what we had been given. Your Son became human like one of us. Look on our frailties with compassion and draw us nearer our Savior, bring us ever deeper into the divine life we were made to share. On the Last Day, we pray you will look on us and see in us the face of Christ Jesus, our only Lord and Redeemer. In his name, we pray. Amen.

Psalm Litanies

These litanies can also be prayed as a novena. Pray one psalm each day, alternating the types of psalms and adding your intentions in the opening prayer.

PENITENTIAL PSALM LITANIES

Penitential Litany I (Ps 6)

In the name of the Father (+)...

Opening Prayer

O Lord, we have turned away from your love, walking the path of disobedience to despair. The way before is dark and we are filled with terror. We are weary of our sin and seek your mercy. Turn, O Lord, and heal us. Amen.

Turn, O Lord, and heal us.

Do not rebuke us in your anger; spare us your righteous wrath.
Be merciful, for we are grieving; our bones break in mourning.
Deliver us from the grave of sin; in death we cannot praise you.
Rescue us from all liars and thieves; we belong to you alone.
Lift the yoke of our burden; free our hands for praise.
Wash us clean of our faults; cover us in your virtue.
Bend us from our vicious ways; set us right on your way.
Relieve us of our despair; show us again your glory.
Reclaim our spirits; take command of our lives.
And we will prosper on the road to righteousness.

Our Father *(together)*

Closing Prayer

O Lord, we fear nothing more than offending you. With hardened hearts and clouded minds, we fall into disobedience and despair. Hear our pleas for mercy! Set your Blessed Mother before us as our guide and grace us with all we need for repentance. In your holy name, we pray. Amen.

Penitential Litany II (Ps 130)

In the name of the Father (+)...

Opening Prayer

Mighty God, you hear the cries of the sinner and show your face to all who repent and do penance. We come to you now, confessing our crimes against your truth. All our faults lie open to your light. My soul waits for you, O Lord. Amen.

My soul waits for you, O Lord.

From the depths of our sin, we wait for you.

From the ways of wicked deceit, hear our cries for rescue.

From unruly minds and cold hearts, hear our cries for rescue.

From the fires of lust and anger, hear our cries for rescue.

From the perils of foolish pride, hear our cries for rescue.

From the pit of gluttony and greed, hear our cries for rescue.

From the prison of envy and despair, hear our cries for rescue.

From the destruction of vengeance, hear our cries for rescue.

From the chains of gossip and detraction, hear our cries for rescue.

And in your wisdom deliver us from darkness.

Our Father *(together)*

Closing Prayer

Mighty and eternal God, your ways are right and true. We have strayed from the flock of your Son. Hear our cries for rescue. Bring us once again into the fold as your holy family and hold us close to your loving care. With your Holy Spirit you blessed the Virgin Mary in her faithful obedience. Bless us with the grace to follow your will and abide in your glory. In your holy name, we pray. Amen.

Penitential Litany III (Ps 143)

In the name of the Father (+)...

Opening Prayer

Father, you are the righteous judge of all your creatures. Weigh against our transgressions the sacrifice of your Son on the cross. Look upon the faith of your Church and forgive us our sins. With humble and contrite hearts, we repent.

With humble and contrite hearts, we repent.

On your altar of mercy, we place before you all our inequities.

On your altar of love, we place before you all our anxieties.

On your altar of forgiveness, we place before you all our betrayals.

On your altar of righteousness, we place before you all our crimes.

On your altar of compassion, we place before you all faint hearts.

On your altar of truth, we place before you all our deceptions.
On your altar of beauty, we place before you all our offenses.
On your altar of goodness, we place before you all our evils.
And before your Sacred Heart, we place our eternal lives.

Our Father *(together)*

Closing Prayer

Father, our hearts grow faint at the thought of offending you. Do not judge your servants according to our sins, but look upon the cross of Christ. Stretch out your hands and water our blistering souls. Save us from the wiles of the enemy and in your steadfast love hide us from temptation. In your holy name, we pray. Amen.

Psalm Litanies of Thanksgiving

Thanksgiving Litany I (Ps 100)

In the name of the Father (+)...

Opening Prayer

Generous and loving God, we enter your temple to give thanks and praise for your blessings. We lift the joyful noise of our praise with gladness and gratitude! You made us. We are your people. Into your presence we come singing and laughing. We give thanks and bless your name. Amen.

We give thanks and bless your name.

All the world, make music for the Lord, singing his praise

All the world, delight in the Lord, shouting for joy.

All the world, exalt in his presence, dancing at his altar of sacrifice.

All the world, cheer his mighty works, feasting at his rich table.

All the world, extol his courts, rejoicing in his righteous mercy.

All the world, magnify his glory, shining out his celestial beauty.

All the world, acclaim his good news, preaching the Word of Life.

All the world, celebrate his favor, harvesting his boundless blessings.

All the world, come to him, kneeling before his heavenly throne.

And revel in the freedom of his children forever!

Our Father *(together)*

Closing Prayer

Generous and loving God, we come into your presence as your people and your nation. You are our rock and our foundation, our shelter in times both bountiful and scarce. We thank you and we bless you for all your gifts. Help us follow your Blessed Mother in magnifying your glory. In your holy name, we pray. Amen.

Thanksgiving Litany II (Ps 95)

In the name of the Father (+)...

Opening Prayer

God above all gods, you alone are holy; you alone are King; you alone are Creator and Lord. We kneel before you as our only Father, our only Savior. Holy Spirit of love and compassion, hear us as we send our thanks and praise to you. We honor all you have given us. Amen.

We honor all you have given us.

For day and night, sun and moon, we thank you.

For sky and sea, wind and wave, we thank you.

For soil and sand, harvest and hardship, we thank you.

For tree and plant, mountain and valley, we thank you.

For fall and winter, leaves and snow, we thank you.

For summer and spring, heat and rain, we thank you.

For birds and animals, fish and insect, we thank you.

For word and song, poetry and praise, we thank you.

For cymbal and drum, dance and science, we thank you.

For all your people: birth, life, death, and life eternal, we thank you.

Our Father *(together)*

Closing Prayer

Creating Father, from nothing you brought forth everything that is and will be. From the dust of the earth and the breath of your mouth, you created us to give you thanks and praise. We honor with our lives all you have made. Only God, only Savior, in your creation your face is revealed to all with eyes to see. For this, and for our salvation through Christ, we worship you and give you thanks. In your holy name, we pray. Amen.

Thanksgiving Litany III (Ps 111)

In the name of the Father (+)...

Opening Prayer

Lord of nations and peoples, we delight in your inheritance, all you have left us to grow in holiness. In the company of angels and saints, we gather to give you thanks for family, friends, neighbors, strangers, and the outcast. With one heart and one voice, we honor the majesty of your works among us. Give thanks to the Lord with your whole heart. Amen.

Give thanks to the Lord with your whole heart.
Delight in his great works among us.
Give him thanks for mothers and fathers.
Give him thanks for sons and daughters.
Give him thanks for grandmothers and grandfathers.
For family, friends, and neighbors, give him thanks.
For the strangers among us, for the foreigner, give him thanks.
For the outcast, the oppressed, the forgotten, give him thanks.
For the just and faithful, the righteous and holy, give him thanks.
And for his covenant of love in Christ and his Church, give him thanks.

Our Father *(together)*

Closing Prayer

Lord, you are King of all nations and all peoples. Under your righteous hand, we are one heart and one voice for the justice you demand. For the love and comfort of family, friends, and neighbors, we give you thanks. We give you thanks and praise for the chance to grow in holiness by being a friend to the stranger, the outcast, and the oppressed. Trusting only in your wisdom, we seek the righteousness of your justice. In your holy name, we pray. Amen.

Part Four

The Beatitude Rosary

The Beatitude Rosary

Praying this rosary and meditating on the mysteries of blessedness will bring you closer to the heart of Christ's teaching found in his Sermon on the Mount. Jesus teaches us that we find his happiness through humility, repentance, and charity.

When we are persecuted for preaching his Word, we are to respond by relying solely on the grace of his Holy Spirit to give us the words for making peace. When we confront our own pride, obstinacy, and apathy, we are bound in obedience to repent and seek reconciliation. Our happiness in Christ is not assured by being right or powerful or feared. We inherit the kingdom when we face insult, persecution, and lies with gladness, charity, and mercy.

The following prayer is designed for a ten-decade rosary. To pray it with a five-decade rosary, use each set of ten beads twice or pray five decades on alternating days.

Crucifix: **Sign of the Cross (+)**

Beatitude Promise *(together)*

Poor in spirit, we weep for our sins and rejoice in Christ's comfort; we hunger and thirst for his righteousness and submit ourselves to his teaching. Longing to be merciful and pure of heart, we strive to be peacemakers for his sake even in the midst of persecution. Amen.

Leader: Lord Jesus, gathering your faithful disciples around you, you taught them the Way of Blessedness, our path to happiness here on earth and in the life to come. Hear us as we follow your Way in prayer and bless us with all the gifts we need to enjoy the beauty made manifest in your Blessed Mother. Lead us to your Sacred Heart, where our eyes will see and our ears will hear. Amen.

(*Bead 1, together*) Our Father…

(*Beads 2, 3, and 4, together*) Mother Mary, Blessed of God, bearer of the Word made flesh, from your virgin womb came Christ Jesus, the Lord, our way to heavenly peace. Be with us now and when we stray. Amen.

(*Bead 5, leader*) Happy are those who follow the path of humility and hope. Happy are those who carry the cross of Christ for his sake. Happy are we who pray for his gift of peace.

FIRST DECADE
Blessedness

Leader: From his abundant goodness, the Lord provides all we need for our happiness.

Meditation
The perfectly lived Christian life is a life of happiness and peace. We might think this means that no Christian will ever suffer from sadness or bouts of turmoil. Not so. The happiness Christ promises to his followers is not a placid serenity or the unmovable calm of a Zen Buddhist monk sitting in meditation.

Rather, Christian happiness is the peace we feel when we know the path we follow leads to the perfection of our purpose as lovers of God. Happiness now depends entirely on our trust in the happiness to come in heaven.

Practically speaking, this means that any sadness we feel, any turmoil we experience, pales beside the grand drama of our eternal lives in God in heaven. Christ and his Church are the rock from which we venture out into the world. Securely anchored to the faith of the Body, we can be at perfect peace knowing that nothing on this earth can come between God and his people. The Sermon on the Mount teaches us exactly what this peace entails and how we not only maintain our hold on God but strengthen that hold as well.

Each beatitude gives us an attitude to adopt and a course of action to take. Faithfully followed, they will bring us closer and closer to the ideal of the perfect Christian life. Thanks be to God that we do not tread the Way of Christ alone! God's treasury of grace is inexhaustible, boundless, and given to us without condition. Though freely given, we must receive these graces to put them to work.

To receive God's gifts, we have only to dispose our hearts and minds to believe and practice the virtues contained in the beatitudes. The exercise of graced virtue builds spiritual muscle and makes the journey to Christ's perfection less strenuous on the soul and more likely to succeed. However, if the journey is taken alone—without family, friends, neighbors, the Church—the stress of carrying the cross will end in defeat.

In all the beatitudes, Jesus clearly indicates that it is the Church being Christ together that is blessed with the kingdom and the earth as their inheritance.

(Ten beads, together) Mother Mary, Blessed of God, bearer of the Word made flesh, from your virgin womb came Christ Jesus, the Lord, our way to heavenly peace. Be with us now and when we stray. Amen.

Beatitude Promise *(together)*

SECOND DECADE

Blessedness of a poor spirit

Leader: "Blessed are the poor in spirit, for theirs is the kingdom of heaven."

Meditation

A common feature of murder-mystery novels is the presumptuous heir, the child or wife or brother who presumes he or she is the heir to the murdered millionaire's fortune. Suspicious minds begin to calculate the ways in which the puffed-up fortune-seeker might have helped their benefactor into the afterlife before his time. The detective-hero often pesters the heir until a better suspect comes along.

In the meantime, most everyone seems content to assume that the one with the most to gain by the death of the millionaire is the one who killed him. With this assumption goes all the gossip, taunts, and derision those left out of the will can muster.

The presumptive heir would be better served by being poor in spirit and assuming nothing about the inheritance. Jesus teaches those gathered that the kingdom of God falls to those who live in worship and awe of the Father, not in prideful spite or the audacious pursuit of worldly kingdoms.

The poor spirit is not bereft of fire or lacking in zeal. Jesus isn't telling us to take on the spirit of a whipped stray found in a dumpster. The spiritual poverty we seek is the humility found in the one who knows that his very life is totally dependent on the love of God.

A humble Christian remembers she is made from the dirt of the earth and given life by the breath of the Creator. Without the loving will of God to bring us up from the ash, we would not be. And absent God's love for us after our creation, we would cease to be.

Knowing this truth, living in the knowledge of our origins and what we would be without divine love, we should nourish a rich sense of humility and uproot any opposing audacity that threatens to choke out God's light. Yes, we are heirs to the kingdom if we are poor in spirit. But this isn't a cause for prideful boasting. Quite the opposite—as humble heirs to the fortunes of merit amassed through the cross, we are grateful and rejoice in our good favor.

(Ten beads, together) Mother Mary, Blessed of God, bearer of the Word made flesh, from your virgin womb came Christ Jesus, the Lord, our way to heavenly peace. Be with us now and when we stray. Amen.

Beatitude Promise *(together)*

THIRD DECADE

Blessedness of weeping

Leader: "Blessed are those who mourn, for they will be comforted."

Meditation

We've all wept. Wept for joy at the birth of a child. Wept in mourning at the death of a loved one. Perhaps we've even wept at others' misfortunes. There is no dearth of occasions for weeping in this world. It seems as though we barely emerge from one deadly disaster only to be plunged back into another, deadlier crisis.

Some might say tears don't challenge injustice. Weeping won't repair war. We can cry and the world turns anyway, spinning as it always has, with us clinging to order and what happiness we can find. True enough. Weeping for the passing of the transient things and people of this world will not restore them. Homes destroyed by flood or fire. Sons and daughters killed in war. Children lost to disease or murder. They will not come back to us simply because we cry for their return. We cry because we must mourn. We must feel the loss and mark it. Give the absence a memorial, a monument.

Christians know the natural world rises from the push and pull of life and death, chaos and structure. We know that what we have and what we are will not always be. We also know the natural world is no product of accident or chance. We live humbly in a vast and complex creation given to us by a loving God. We live *in* this world, but we cannot be *of* it. We can live in his creation because we are his children, intimately bound as creatures of dust to everything he composed from nothing.

But to be *of the world* means we cling to the things his frail creatures have made, to claim a stake in the world of artifice and invention. When we take up the cross and follow Christ, this world falls away and we can mourn it. And when we do, we are comforted by God's Holy Spirit, because even though we no longer live as men and women of the world, we haven't yet found ourselves among the beauties of heaven.

The blessedness promised isn't that we'll never grieve, but that the Love who created us will be with us always.

(Ten beads, together) Mother Mary, Blessed of God, bearer of the Word made flesh, from your virgin womb came Christ Jesus, the Lord, our way to heavenly peace. Be with us now and when we stray. Amen.

Beatitude Promise *(together)*

FOURTH DECADE

Blessedness of seeking righteousness

Leader: "Blessed are those who hunger and thirst for righteousness, for they will be filled."

Meditation

Hungering and thirsting after righteousness is dangerous. The moment we recognize the desire to live in right relationship with God, we place ourselves perilously close to final failure. The chasm between God's righteousness and our independent ability to join ours with his is infinite, uncrossable. No amount of work, sacrifice, prayer, or wealth can fill the valley that separates us from the holiness of God.

So why do we hunger and thirst for what we can't have? Why do we long for love and peace that never comes? From this side of the chasm—our human side—the holiness we desire is unreachable, forever out of our grasp. Nothing we can invent, make, conceive, or discover will propel us into righteousness.

What can we construct from the impermanent world that will itself not be impermanent? What can we discover in creation that is not itself made? Nothing. So why are we so naturally disposed to seek the fulfillment of a purpose, to achieve a goal that cannot by its very nature be satisfied by our works? Our hunger and thirst for righteousness are gifts, graced deficiencies in our souls that drive us to the one who can and will satisfy all our longings.

Architects and engineers could rightly say of this world that it's designed for obsolescence; it was made to be replaced in time, designed to be old-fashioned and useless when we come to consider our divine end. Light bulbs, car parts, relationships—all serve their proper purpose, but they must be changed out, replaced when they fail.

As soon as we understand that nothing around us will fill our need for righteousness, for a right relationship with God, we clearly see how obsolete made-things are in satisfying the hunger and thirst we've been given. At this instant of clarity, we are blessed. And we are blessed to seek the eternal food and drink of heaven.

(Ten beads, together) Mother Mary, Blessed of God, bearer of the Word made flesh, from your virgin womb came Christ Jesus, the Lord, our way to heavenly peace. Be with us now and when we stray. Amen.

Beatitude Promise *(together)*

FIFTH DECADE
Blessedness of the meek

Leader: "Blessed are the meek, for they will inherit the earth."

Meditation

Say the word *meek* out loud several times. To me, *meek* evokes both the image and sound of a mouse—small, squeaky, scurrying around, trying to hide. You probably have someone in your family or among your friends whom you would describe as meek and mild, someone who stands back from the press of the crowd or likes to spend time alone and never gets upset or speaks up with an opinion. The meek and mild are easily bullied, simply swayed.

Meek also makes me think of shyness, introversion, timidity, and passivity. Not at all the type of person who would survive a disaster or wade through a crisis to come out in the end as the heir to the earth. How are the meek blessed? Why would being passive or timid bring us closer to happiness?

Traditionally, Christian meekness has been thought of as a kind of docility in the face of persecution. Just take the licking and keep on praying for your oppressors. This isn't wrong, just incomplete. Just as there are more ways of doing violence to your soul than outright mortally sinning, there are more ways to be properly meek than adopting a radical pacifism in the face of violence.

One of the most dangerous ways we risk the integrity of our souls is by standing stubbornly against the teachings of Christ and his Church. Having made up our minds about some issue or another, we shut your hearts and minds to further persuasion. No additional information, argument, experience, or authority will alter our stand. We might think this sort of stubbornness is a virtue when it comes to holding to the revelations of Scripture or the truth of dogma.

However, so long as we live we're subject to growing in understanding through instruction and experience. Meekness isn't an order to stand ready to compromise the truth, but rather a way to peace by remaining intellectually and spiritually pliable in the hands of Christ and his Church.

A faithful heart docile enough to be taught anew can let error flow through and out while keeping the clarity of truth intact. A heart stubbornly closed against instruction can only harbor truth and error together in a murky mix that soon festers.

The meek inherit the earth because they allow truth to flush out evil.

(Ten beads, together) Mother Mary, Blessed of God, bearer of the Word made flesh, from your virgin womb came Christ Jesus, the Lord, our way to heavenly peace. Be with us now and when we stray. Amen.

Beatitude Promise *(together)*

SIXTH DECADE

Blessedness of mercy

Leader: "Blessed are the merciful, for they will receive mercy."

Meditation

When we pray the Our Father, we pray God will forgive our sins in the same way we forgive the sins of others. This is wonderful news if you're inclined to easily forgive those who have sinned against you. But if you're prone to holding grudges or seeking revenge, you might want to meditate on the Our Father and ask yourself whether you want God to treat your sins in the same way you treat others' sins.

Mercy works much the same way. When we show mercy, we are blessed with mercy and we become merciful, filled with mercy. Surely this is a vital element to our happiness here on earth. It is. But why? Think about when you hear the word *mercy* in everyday life. Maybe you've heard it said on a TV crime drama that a convicted criminal is going to throw himself on the mercy of the court. The convict's attorney will plea before the judge for the mildest punishment allowable by law. If the judge is merciful, she will hear the plea, sentence the convict according to law, and then reduce the sentence or suspend it entirely.

For Christians, one element of this everyday use of *mercy* makes sense and another does not. Before mercy can be shown, the criminal must be convicted of a crime and sentenced. Likewise, for a Christian, God's mercy is applied only after justice has been done. In other words, we're first found guilty of our sin, sentenced, and then shown mercy.

For the criminal, mercy is an option. For sinners, mercy is a guarantee. Christ's sacrifice on the cross satisfied divine justice, making us right before the judgment seat. Whatever we owe God for our sins has been paid in full by Christ. We have already been shown mercy. Therefore, showing mercy to those who sin against us is one way we express gratitude to God for his patience with our own sins. Blessedness thrives in mercy because the merciful don't count costs or collect debt, nor do they lend their love or borrow from others. Mercy is freely given and freely received.

(Ten beads, together) Mother Mary, Blessed of God, bearer of the Word made flesh, from your virgin womb came Christ Jesus, the Lord, our way to heavenly peace. Be with us now and when we stray. Amen.

Beatitude Promise *(together)*

SEVENTH DECADE

Blessedness of a pure heart

Leader: "Blessed are the pure in heart, for they will see God."

Meditation

If you wear glasses, you know the aggravation that comes with smudgy or fogged-up lenses. It's the same aggravation as when heavy rain pounds your windshield and obscures your vision or if you have to walk around in a dark house risking the health of your toes.

Those of us who see (even poorly!) can barely imagine what it must be like to be blind. What is it like to never see color or shape or depth? The world becomes a very different place of subtle sounds, small textures, intense flavors, and large, trailing scents.

Whatever the sighted imagine the world of the blind to be, they cannot say the blind don't see God. Though we will come to see God face-to-face, while we are here on this earth we see him with the eyes of our heart, not the eyes in our head. But if you think this means we know God most intimately through our affections, think again.

In the Christian tradition, the heart is the seat of the soul, the throne upon which the image and likeness of God sits. The heart is the center of our being, the altar for our worship, the tabernacle where the Divine Presence rules. When the heart is restless, worried, distracted, or clogged with sin, our vision of God is obscured, muddled. We find ourselves off-kilter, preoccupied with trivialities, unable to pray, stressed to the breaking point. As we do with our glasses, we must occasionally clean our hearts of smudges, fog, grime, and sin, scrub at the stuck-on spots, maybe even think about replacing the worn, scratched-up heart for a newer, fresher one.

The Son came to us as a man so we might see with hearts renewed, refreshed, and restored. *Whom* we see is not new. *How* we see him is. Purity of heart is more than good moral behavior and right belief. Behaving well and believing rightly are products of a clear vision of who God is for us. The image and likeness resting in our hearts speaks to the One whose image and likeness they are. If, as the psalms say, deep roars to deep, then we can say that God shows us his Sacred Heart beating in our human hearts. And we see.

(Ten beads, together) Mother Mary, bearer of the Word made flesh, from your virgin womb came Christ Jesus the Lord, our way to heavenly peace. Be with us now and when we stray. Amen.

Beatitude Promise *(together)*

EIGHTH DECADE

Blessedness of making peace

Leader: "Blessed are the peacemakers, for they will be called children of God."

Meditation

Most of us know how to make a pot of coffee or a sandwich. Many of us know how to make a casserole or a paper snowflake. Some of us even know how to make bread pudding and homemade pasta. But how many of us know how to make peace?

Shoved hard enough and insulted vigorously enough, most of us could probably be roused to make war. Without much shoving or insult, many of us gladly work to make money. Some of us could even be persuaded to make a deal. But how many of us will follow an order to make peace?

This beatitude is probably the most hotly contested of the eight Jesus taught. At different times and in different places, it has been used as a justification for absolute pacifism during wartime and nonviolent resistance in civil disobedience. Traditionally, Christians have followed Saint Augustine's interpretation of what it means to be a peacemaker. In his work "On the Sermon on the Mount," Augustine argues that a child of God should be like his Father in every way possible. This means subjecting the child's tumultuous passions to the rule of reason. When the child's carnal desires are properly tamed, there is peace in his spiritual kingdom, making him more like his Father than before.

Augustine sees this taming process as a matter of allowing superior reason to tame and rule inferior passion. If we understand peace as more than merely the absence of passion or violence, then we must understand peace as something made, something brought about. Not an absence, but a real presence. And that real presence is the friendship of Christ among his own people and anyone else who values right reason, putting aside hatred, violence, vengeance, and wrath.

We do know how to make peace so long as we remember how to make friends. If the peaceful heart is the father of a friendship, then the friendship will grow in the peace of the Father.

(Ten beads, together) Mother Mary, Blessed of God, bearer of the Word made flesh, from your virgin womb came Christ Jesus, the Lord, our way to heavenly peace. Be with us now and when we stray. Amen.

Beatitude Promise *(together)*

NINTH DECADE
Blessedness of the persecuted

Leader: "Blessed are those who are persecuted for righteousness' sake, for theirs is the kingdom of heaven."

Meditation

You've probably seen the t-shirt that reads, "Just Because I'm Paranoid Doesn't Mean They Aren't Out to Get Me!" A joke, of course, but one that portrays the idea that persecution doesn't have to be obvious or even real to be genuinely felt. We've all been snubbed, insulted, humiliated; you may even have been physically attacked or jailed for a real or imagined offense.

Few in the western world have been truly persecuted, violently harassed in the Biblical sense of being persecuted for the faith. Christ promises his disciples that they will follow him on the road to sorrow and death. He doesn't hide or downplay the dangers of preaching the Gospel.

When we stand against the spirit of the world, that spirit—disobedient, devious, raging mad—pushes back. In western liberal democracies, the worst sorts of persecutions are mitigated by law and custom; we are cushioned against the more deadly forms of opposition to the Gospel because our nations are founded on principles of liberty and reason. Not all Christians are so blessed.

What this means for us is that the persecution of the Church takes on more subtle forms, equally diabolical but not as obviously violent or deadly. In fact, so subtle are some forms of persecution that Christians persecute other Christians, believing all the while that what they do is perfectly moral. Jesus warned that the Gospel would raise the hand of brother against brother and set families at war.

But why are those who are persecuted especially blessed with God's happiness? What's so *happy* about being persecuted? Essential to the perfection of the Christian life is the imitation of Christ on his way to the cross. If we are to *become* Christ, we must *follow* Christ. Not just following his instructions like we would follow a recipe, but following in his footsteps, doing what he did and having done to us what was done to him. Being beaten bloody by the police and executed on false charges are not prerequisites for entering heaven, but being willing and ready to be is.

Pray none of us is given the chance to prove the strength of our hearts. And pray that if the chance comes anyway, we have the fortitude to bear under and follow Christ to our cross.

(Ten beads, together) Mother Mary, Blessed of God, bearer of the Word made flesh, from your virgin womb came Christ Jesus, the Lord, our way to heavenly peace. Be with us now and when we stray. Amen.

Beatitude Promise *(together)*

TENTH DECADE
Blessedness of rejoicing

Leader: "Rejoice and be glad, for your reward is great in heaven."

Meditation

Many contemporary philosophers and theologians argue that human language and image are woefully inadequate to express or represent the true nature of God.

This isn't a new discovery. Moses knew this when he came upon the burning bush and God told him not to look upon his face because doing so would strike Moses dead. The glory of God is too much, in excess of, over and above anything we can ever comprehend this side of heaven. God tells Moses that his name is "I AM THAT I AM." Not a being like Moses, but Being himself, the pure act of existence.

We can write that sentence. We may even have some limited understanding of what it means. What we can never do is exhaust the divine nature in word or image. God forbade Moses from making graven images of him precisely because all such images would be lies. So, are we left speechless when it comes time to talk about God? How do we express the deepest longings for God except in words and pictures?

We rejoice! If we cannot describe, draw, compose, carve, paint, or build our longings for God, we rejoice. We praise. Without words or images, we praise God for his blessings and his bounty. We can read a psalm or we can sing it. If we sing, we pray twice, Augustine assures us. Words of praise can be written or composed; images of praise can be painted or drawn. But praise itself is the act of purest worship, wholly giving over to the Spirit all we have to give. Praise is jubilation and cheering and crying out and applauding and celebrating.

We Catholics shy away from this sort of emotional display. We are familiar with reverence, dignity, and solemn prayer; but praising God in the way the disciples did at Pentecost makes us profoundly uncomfortable. Can't we just rejoice quietly back here on the last pew? As a matter of fact, we can.

Our deepest delights in God's presence can be expressed in the elation of a heart made pure by grace. Visible expression is well and good, but the clean heart and pure mind can just as readily celebrate in the silence and stillness of a child brought to Christ for his mercy. When we rejoice, we bring ourselves fully to the throne of God. All our words, images, dancing, shouting, clapping—everything comes with us and hears us clearly as his elated children.

(Ten beads, together) Mother Mary, Blessed of God, bearer of the Word made flesh, from your virgin womb came Christ Jesus, the Lord, our way to heavenly peace. Be with us now and when we stray. Amen.

Beatitude Promise *(together)*

Sources and Permissions

English translation of *Catechism of the Catholic Church* for the United States of America, Second Edition 1994. Copyright © 1994, United States Catholic Conference, Inc.—Libreria Editrice Vaticana. English translation of the *Catechism of the Catholic Church*: Modifications from the Editio Typica copyright © 1997, United States Catholic Conference, Inc.—Libreria Editrice Vaticana.

Excerpts from *Meister Eckhart: The Essential Sermons, Commentaries, Treatises, and Defense*, translated and introduced by Edmund Colledge, O.S.A. and Bernard McGinn. Copyright © 1981 by Paulist Press, Paulist Press, Inc., New York/ Mahwah, NJ. Reprinted by permission of Paulist Press, Inc.

Excerpts from *Gregory of Nyssa: The Life of Moses*, translation, introduction and notes by Everett Ferguson and Abraham J. Malherbe. Copyright © 1978 by Paulist Press, Paulist Press, Inc., New York/Mahwah, NJ. Reprinted by permission of Paulist Press, Inc.

English translation excerpt from Mystical Theology is from *Dionysius the Areopagite: The Mystical Theology and the Celestial Hierarchies,* 17-19.

English translation excerpt from The Divine Names is from *The Works of Dionysius the Areopagite,* transl. by Rev. John Parker, M.A., (London: James Parker and Co., 1897).

"Hymn to the Transcendence of God" is a revised version of a the hymn shown in *On What Cannot Be Said: Apophatic Discourses in Philosophy, Religion, Literature, and the Arts,* vol. 1, William Franke, ed., University of Notre Dame Press, 2007, p. x.

Certain quotes from these Church fathers—Augustine, Clement of Alexandria, Cyril of Jerusalem, Ephraim the Syrian, Gregory Nazianzen, Gregory of Nyssa, Gregory the Wonderworker (Gregory Thaumaturgus), Hilary of Poitiers, and John of Damascus—are used with permission from www.newadvent.org/ fathers/, courtesy of Kevin Knight. The quotes are derived from *Nicene and Post-Nicene Fathers, First Series,* Vol. 3, transl. Arthur West Haddan, ed. Philip Schaff. (Buffalo, NY: Christian Literature Publishing Co., 1887.) Revised and edited for New Advent by Kevin Knight.

About the Author

Fr. Philip Neri Powell, OP, is a Dominican friar of the Province of St. Martin de Porres (USA). He teaches philosophy of nature, religion, and science at the Pontifical University of St. Thomas Aquinas in Rome and classical western theology and literature at the University of Dallas in Irving, Texas. His most recent book for Liguori Publications, *Treasures Old and New*, was published in 2009.